LOVERS' LEAP

A Comedy in Three Acts

BY

PHILIP JOHNSON

Copyright, 1934, by Philip Johnson
Copyright (Acting Edition), 1935, by Philip Johnson

All rights reserved

SAMUEL FRENCH LIMITED
LONDON

Copyright © 1934 by Philip Johnson
Copyright (Acting Edition) © 1935 by Philip Johnson
All Rights Reserved

LOVERS' LEAP is fully protected under the copyright laws of the British Commonwealth, including Canada, the United States of America, and all other countries of the Copyright Union.

All rights, including professional and amateur stage productions, recitation, lecturing, public reading, motion picture, radio broadcasting, television and the rights of translation into foreign languages are strictly reserved.

ISBN 978-0-573-11490-8

www.samuelfrench.co.uk
www.samuelfrench.com

FOR AMATEUR PRODUCTION ENQUIRIES

UNITED KINGDOM AND WORLD EXCLUDING NORTH AMERICA

plays@samuelfrench.co.uk
020 7255 4302/01

Each title is subject to availability from Samuel French, depending upon country of performance.

CAUTION: Professional and amateur producers are hereby warned that LOVERS' LEAP is subject to a licensing fee. Publication of this play does not imply availability for performance. Both amateurs and professionals considering a production are strongly advised to apply to the appropriate agent before starting rehearsals, advertising, or booking a theatre. A licensing fee must be paid whether the title is presented for charity or gain and whether or not admission is charged.

No one shall make any changes in this title for the purpose of production. No part of this book may be reproduced, stored in a retrieval system, or transmitted in any form, by any means, now known or yet to be invented, including mechanical, electronic, photocopying, recording, videotaping, or otherwise, without the prior written permission of the publisher. No one shall upload this title, or part of this title, to any social media websites.

The right of Philip Johnson to be identified as author of this work has been asserted by him in accordance with Section 77 of the Copyright, Designs and Patents Act 1988.

LOVERS' LEAP

First produced at the Playhouse, Liverpool, on June 1st, 1934, with the following cast of characters:

HELEN STORER	Ena Burrill.
POYNTER	Harry Andrews.
SARAH TRAILLE	Lindisfarne Hamilton.
CEDRIC NORREYS	James Stephenson.
ROGER STORER	Wyndham Goldie.

The Play produced by WILLIAM ARMSTRONG.

And subsequently at the Vaudeville Theatre, Strand, London, on October 25th, 1934, with the following cast of characters:

(In the order of their appearance)

HELEN STORER	Nora Swinburne.
POYNTER	John Counsell.
SARAH TRAILLE	Ursula Jeans.
CEDRIC NORREYS	Walter Hudd.
ROGER STORER	Owen Nares.

The Play produced by OWEN NARES.

The action of the play takes place at Helen's house in the country, between four o'clock of an afternoon in June and ten o'clock the next morning.

LOVERS' LEAP

ACT I

SCENE.—HELEN'S *house in the country.*
The room is of moderate size, with double doors L. *leading into the dining-room, and double doors* R. *admitting to the library.* L.C. *back is a wide arched opening, beyond which, on a higher level and achieved by two broad steps, is the entrance-hall of the house. The scheme of furnishing and decoration is charming, and conveys an immediate impression of originality and discrimination. The walls, including those of the entrance-hall beyond, are painted a light cream, while the carpets on both the floors are of some pale neutral shade. This restraint in the use of any predominating colour is observed in the upholstery and cushions, the one really brilliant-hued note being obtained by the curtains over the arched openings* R. *and* L. *in the hall. Slightly* R. *of* C. *in the room is a fairly long refectory table, and below this, but a little to the* R., *a settee. Set against the* R. *wall below the door is a sideboard, and below this a desk with stool. On the other side, almost against the* L. *wall, is a baby grand piano, and in the corner down* L. *a radio-gramophone. Stairs* R.C. *lead to the first floor, and there is a window back* C. *on the rostrum looking on to the garden. Chairs are distributed about the room at the discretion of the producer. The room has the appearance of being used as the common-room of the house : there are papers and magazines strewn on the refectory table, also a cigarette-box and ashtrays.*
(*See Ground Plan of Scene.*)

When the CURTAIN *rises it is the afternoon of a day in June.* HELEN STORER *is standing down* C., *her back to the audience, glancing from the refectory table to the piano and back again. She is about thirty-five, alert, attractive and possessed of an excellent figure, and is simply but quite exquisitely dressed in a gown of some soft, clinging material. She goes up to the table, picks up the vase of delphiniums and takes them to the piano, placing the rose-bowl on the armchair* L.C. *Having studied the effect, she decides against the vase and replaces it on the table* R.C., *then goes to the armchair for the rose-bowl. She upsets some water on the seat of the armchair and, after taking the bowl to the piano, comes back and wipes it off with her handkerchief. She looks round the room, then goes to the piano and looks at herself in the mirror on the* L. *wall. She suddenly thinks of the photograph, crosses to the desk* R., *searches for it, finds it, recrosses to the piano, places it there and studies the effect. She decides to ring the bell, and goes to above the door* R. *and does so, then picks up* "*Vogue*" *from the table and sits at* L. *end of the settee. After a moment, deciding against the photograph, she springs up, snatches it from the piano, and thrusts it back into the desk, trapping her finger as she slams the drawer to. She murmurs a* "*damn*," *and at that moment* POYNTER *enters on the rostrum from* R.

POYNTER. You rang, madam?
HELEN. Yes. When the gentleman who is calling this afternoon arrives, show him straight in here.
POYNTER. And not to keep him waiting five minutes, as you said?
HELEN. No. Straight in here.
POYNTER. Very well, madam.

(*As* POYNTER *turns up* C. *and to* R., *the door-bell rings. In response to the bell he turns, recrosses the rostrum and disappears to* L. *The sound of the bell has startled* HELEN *into a half-suppressed gasp. She glances agitatedly round the room, then sits* R. *on the settee, giving a quick, furtive pat at her hair, as* POYNTER, *followed by* SARAH TRAILLE, *enters.* SARAH *is about twenty-eight, very beautiful, with perfect poise, and exquisitely graceful in all her movements. Her clothes are very lovely, and she is wearing a small travelling-hat.*)

(*Announcing.*) Miss Traille, madam.

(*He goes off to* L., *reappears almost immediately carrying a suitcase, recrosses the rostrum, and goes off to* R.)

SARAH (*coming down stage*). Darling, here I am.
HELEN (*in very come-to-earth tones*). Oh—it's you!
SARAH (*halting abruptly*). Aren't you glad to see me? (*Anxiously.*) Helen, you did get my letter this morning?
HELEN (*rising*). Of course I did, and of course I'm glad to see you. Come and kiss me at once.

(*They kiss,* C.)

How marvellous you're looking.
SARAH (*down* L.C.). So are you. (*Referring to* HELEN'S *dress.*) Manell?
HELEN (*nodding*). Like it?
SARAH. Lovely.
HELEN. And how are you?
SARAH. Just numb from head to foot. I drove up from the station in the village taxi.
HELEN. You poor dear. Sit down at once.
SARAH (*going to armchair* L.C.). If I'm still able to. (*She sits.*) Ah, not so bad as I feared.

(HELEN *takes a cigarette-box from the table* R.C. *and offers it to* SARAH.)

She takes one herself, replaces the box on the table, returns to SARAH *and offers her a light. She lights* SARAH's *cigarette and her own, then moves to* C.)

(*Leaning back luxuriously.*) How lovely it is to have a perfectly adorable house in the country! Oh! by the way, Cedric had to spend last night in Winchester, so he's coming on from there by car.

HELEN (*coming down* C.). Cedric? Cedric who?

SARAH (*looking at her*). Why, Cedric Norreys, of course. (*Sitting up.*) Helen, you're quite sure you *did* get my letter?

HELEN. Yes, dear. Yes, of course.

SARAH. Then, when I said I was coming for the week-end, surely I explained that I was bringing Cedric Norreys with me?

HELEN. Cedric Norreys! Oh, of course! How stupid of me!

SARAH (*looking at her rather narrowly*). Darling—you're not ill or anything? Are you?

HELEN (*above* L. *end of settee*). Ill? No. Why, do I look it?

SARAH. There's a curious aura of vagueness about you. (*Rising.*) If it isn't convenient for you to have us, do for goodness' sake say so at once, and I'll invent excuses to Cedric the moment he arrives.

HELEN. Now, don't be ridiculous! I shall love having you—both of you.

(*They kiss.*)

SARAH (*with a relieved sigh*). That's all right, then. (*She sits in the armchair again.*)

HELEN (*with rather elaborate carelessness, moving* R.C.). By the way, I'm expecting someone to tea to-day. (*She sits at* R. *end of settee.*)

SARAH. Are you, dear? A man?

(HELEN *nods.*)

Why didn't you ask him to dinner? So much more a man's meal, and we should have been an even number.

HELEN. Perhaps I'll ask him to stay; that is, if you promise not to be rude to him, Sarah.

SARAH. Helen, it isn't that poisonous creature who was here last time, and talked of nothing but patent manures?

HELEN. It isn't. . . . As a matter of fact—it's Roger.

SARAH (*sitting erect; with an exclamation*). What?

HELEN. Roger, dear.

(SARAH *rises, goes to the* L. *end of the settee, and stares at her blankly.*)

SARAH. Helen, is this a joke? You're not serious!

HELEN. My dear, a husband one hasn't set eyes on for seven years dropping in to tea is no joke.

SARAH (*still unable to grasp the news*). But—but he's in Egypt.

HELEN (*shaking her head*). No, dear, no. I had a letter from him this morning, to say he landed at Southampton yesterday, was buying a car and motoring to Town to-day, calling here on his way.

SARAH (*speechless*). Well . . . of all the . . . (*She turns up stage.*)

HELEN. Yes, I know.

(*There is a very short pause. Then :*)

SARAH (*up* C., *intensely*). Oh, the utter, utter swine! (*She moves down again.*)

HELEN. Sarah, please!

SARAH (*down* C.). How dared he!

HELEN. Well, it's happened, and it's no use lashing ourselves into a state of resentment about it at this stage.

SARAH (L. *of the settee*). But—it's too awful—I mean—what will you say to him?

HELEN. I haven't thought.

SARAH. I should have been thinking of nothing else. You can't just hand the brute a cup of tea and say "What weather." Thank God for one thing, at any rate: Cedric and I will be here to back you up; you won't be quite at his mercy. Why not refuse to see him?

HELEN. Not at home, you mean?

SARAH. Not damn-well at home to you, would be more satisfying.

HELEN (*shaking her head*). I couldn't take that line with a man who merely asks for a cup of tea.

SARAH. I could, if the man who asked for a cup of tea were the man I'd every right to have breakfast in bed with. . . . How can you be so calm about it, Helen? I should be seething! (*She crosses* L. *to the piano.*)

HELEN. I did seethe a little just at first, but it only made me feel rather sick, so I took a couple of aspirins instead.

SARAH (*moving* C. *again*). What sort of a letter was it?

HELEN. Well, it was written on the steamer notepaper. You know, crossed flags at the top.

SARAH. I don't care if it was festooned with bunting. (L. *of the settee.*) What did he say, I mean?

HELEN. Just that he'd like to see me, as he—had something he wished to talk to me about.

SARAH. Helen—supposing it should be—— (*She sits beside her, at* L. *end of the settee.*)

HELEN. Yes, dear?

SARAH. Supposing it should be that—that he wants to come back to you! (*As* HELEN *does not immediately reply.*) Oh, Helen, you'd never do that! You—you couldn't!

(HELEN *rises and moves round* R. *to back of the settee.*)

HELEN (*after a moment*). Don't you think it would be silly of us to start supposing things at this stage?

SARAH. Oh, all right ... (*Rising.*) Only, I hope if he makes any such suggestion, you'll have the presence of mind to smack his stupid face. (*She crosses* L., *picks up her bag from the armchair, puts her hat on the piano, and makes-up at the mirror.*)

HELEN. Roger's face was not stupid; he was extremely good-looking. (*She comes down* C.)

SARAH. Living abroad for seven years will have changed all that. I expect by now he's as yellow as a guinea and as bald as a coot.

HELEN. Oh—don't!

SARAH. Oh! (*Going towards* HELEN, C.) Isn't Egypt where they get that frightful——

HELEN (*interrupting hastily*). Sarah, listen to me. I want you to be very patient and understanding, and to do me a great favour.

SARAH. Darling, anything I can do to help.

HELEN (C.). Then, don't say another word about Roger for at least half an hour. I'm straining every nerve I possess to clamp down my feelings, so as to be able to face this meeting with a little self-possession; but I shall certainly fail to do that if you work me up into a panic beforehand.

SARAH (*reluctantly*). Oh ... all right! I'll hold my tongue until it aches. (*She sits in the armchair* L.C.)

HELEN. There's no need to do that. Let's talk about something else. (*She crosses to below the settee.*)

SARAH. What?

HELEN. Oh—anything.

SARAH. I see. (*After a long pause.*) How are the crops?

HELEN (*down* R. *of the settee*). Do I know them?

SARAH. Crops, dear. Hay and stuff.

HELEN. Oh! I haven't the faintest idea. (*She crosses up to back of the settee.*)

SARAH. Sunk!

(*Another pause. Then:*)

HELEN (*above* L. *end of the settee, brightly*). Tell me all about your Cedric what's-his-name. (*She sits on* L. *arm of the settee.*)

SARAH (*instantly relaxing her attitude*). Cedric Norreys, dear.

HELEN. Where did you meet him?

SARAH. At the Lidyard's cricket week. We slept together through most of the matches, and since then we've met fairly frequently in Town.

HELEN. What's he like?

SARAH. Oh—well ... he's just a man.

HELEN. I'm glad. So many of them aren't these days, I'm told. What's his type?

SARAH. Cedric's quite ordinary really ... except in one tiny detail.

HELEN. And what's that?

SARAH. Well ... he happens to be rather in love with me.

HELEN. I don't see anything so out of the ordinary in that. Lots of other men have been, haven't they?

SARAH. This time, though, it's rather different. Because, you see, I—well—I'm not at all sure that I'm not just a little bit in love with him.

HELEN (*rising with an impulsive movement towards her*). At last! Sarah, darling—you mean that? Seriously? Oh, but this is too wonderful. He isn't married or anything, is he?

SARAH (*shaking her head*). He's almost unbelievably eligible. The sort of unexciting nice looks that grow on one, nephew of the Duke of St. Donat's and absurdly rich.

HELEN. And he's in love with you? He's told you so?

SARAH. Told me so! He's whispered it, he's crooned it, and he's shouted it.

HELEN (*sitting on the* R. *arm of her chair—delighted*). Oh, Sarah, dearest! I can't tell you how glad I am! (*About to kiss her, then drawing back.*) He—he has asked you to marry him, of course?

SARAH (*rising before she answers*). Oh, yes, he's asked me to marry him. (*She goes to the piano and picks up her hat.*)

HELEN. That's all right, then. One never knows, these days. (*After a pause.*) Well, you're going to accept him, aren't you?

(SARAH *moves a little down* L. *to the end of the piano.*)

SARAH. I don't know, Helen—yet. (*She replaces her hat on the piano.*)

HELEN (*rising*). You don't know? (*Taking a step towards her.*) But—if he loves you, and you love him!

SARAH. I know. (*Moving up and* R.) It sounds perfectly simple, doesn't it?

HELEN (*going to her and taking her down* R., *below the settee*). Now, darling, I do hope you're not going to be foolish about this. It's been very nice for you to have your little flat in Town, all gay and independent; but you wouldn't like to think that life was never going to mean any more to you than that. . . . I mean, Sarah, you're not growing any—well—any—after all, you're twenty-eight.

SARAH. Old enough not to muddle any good chance that may come along? You needn't worry, dearest; I'm not going to muddle this one. (*She sits at* R. *end of the settee.*)

HELEN. Then—you're going to accept him? (*She sits at* L. *end of the settee.*)

SARAH. Quite definitely. I like my little Cedric very much.

HELEN. But—I thought you said——

SARAH (*laughing*). Poor darling Helen, looking all bewildered.

HELEN. You're being very exasperating, Sarah.

SARAH. Now listen, Helen: when Cedric and I decided to spend this week-end with you, it was because we both felt that when a problem has to be grappled with, then the country's the place to do the grappling in.

HELEN. Problem?
SARAH. Yes; of Cedric and Sarah . . . whether it is to be marriage, or—the other thing.
HELEN (*staring at her*). What other thing?
SARAH (*with a short laugh*). My dear!
HELEN (*getting up after a moment—aghast*). You—you don't mean——
SARAH (*nodding*). I do.
HELEN. My God! (*She sits again.*)
SARAH. You see, Helen, we've pledged ourselves to decide during this Saturday to Monday, whether we'll marry or—just live together. (*Continuing, quite unperturbed.*) If by Monday morning we've decided upon marriage, then we shall waste no time; if it is to be the other thing, then we shall waste even less.
HELEN. Sarah!
SARAH. We shall telephone to Paris for a table at dinner, a double bedroom, and leave Croydon by the afternoon plane.
HELEN. You're mad! Quite, quite mad!
SARAH. My dear, if everyone were as sane, the Divorce Court judges would be able to lower their golf handicaps in no time.
HELEN (*rising*). Stop being flippant! (*Beginning to pace up and down.*) You say he's motoring down here, this man?

(SARAH *nods her head.*)

Just wait till I meet him!
SARAH. Let me tell you, my dear, that Cedric is a man of perfectly sound morals.
HELEN. Does a man of perfectly sound morals usually offer a woman the alternative of either marrying him or becoming his mistress?
SARAH. He does not, as Cedric most emphatically pointed out when I made the suggestion.
HELEN. *You* made the suggestion?
SARAH. Of course.

(HELEN *appears to be struggling to speak.*)

HELEN. I'm horrified!
SARAH. So was Cedric. In fact, it may help you to realize just how charming and unspoilt he is when I tell you he blushed, actually blushed, and that his first impulse quite clearly was to refuse.
HELEN. H'm! . . . What was his second?
SARAH. To accept—reluctantly. You see, he really is terribly in love with me.
HELEN. He must be; otherwise he'd have put you over his knee and smacked you.
SARAH. Darling, why not wait until Monday before abandoning me as a total loss? Who knows, after a careful weighing of the pros and cons, we may plump for matrimony, after all?

HELEN. Why do you keep on saying "we" when you know that the whole matter rests entirely with you?

SARAH (*rising to the back of the settee*). Oh, but Cedric, of course, will have his say.

HELEN (*at* R. *end of the settee*). But you've told me that his one ambition is to marry you.

SARAH. Well, so it was, but he's come to realize there's something to be said for my point of view.

HELEN (*turning up* R.). The poor fool!

SARAH (*moving to* R. *end of the settee*). Cedric is not a fool, Helen. He is the one man who, in my estimation, stands head and shoulders above any other man I've ever met.

HELEN (*moving* C.). If that's how you feel about him, then why on earth don't you decide to marry him at once? (*Coming down* C.) Why don't you?

SARAH (*after a moment*). Because I'm afraid. (*She sits on the stool at the desk* R.)

HELEN. Afraid?

SARAH. Of—of marriage.

HELEN (*crossing over to her*). Sarah, you've been reading one of those nasty books.

SARAH. Don't be silly! Not that part of it. . . . I'm afraid of what it may do to both of us.

HELEN. *Do* to you? . . . I don't understand. (*She sits on the* R. *arm of the settee.*)

SARAH. Well, surely, after what happened to you and Roger—— (*She checks herself.*)

HELEN (*starting, then after a tiny pause*). Oh! So that's what it is!

SARAH. Oh, I'm sorry, Helen.

(*There is a fairly long pause. Then* HELEN *rises and goes above settee to* L.)

HELEN (*slowly*). Because of Roger and me.

SARAH (*haltingly*). Darling, I didn't mean to tell you.

HELEN (*turning at the piano*). You must be even madder than I thought.

SARAH (*with sudden defiance*). Why? Because, with your experience in front of me, I choose to look with extra special care before I leap? You see, that's how I've come to look upon the whole business—as a sort of lovers' leap. You may make a perfect landing and go cantering gaily on; or you may come a hell of a cropper. . . .

HELEN. But—how do you know you would?

SARAH. How do I know I wouldn't? I'm a rotten little coward, Helen, when it comes to a gamble—especially when it's my life's happiness at stake.

HELEN (*crossing to* L. *end of the settee*). But, great heavens, you love one another, don't you?

SARAH. Just as you and Roger loved one another—before marriage.
HELEN (*moving round to the back of the settee*). You fool! ... Why, you might as well say you were never going to eat another egg because you once heard of somebody getting a bad one.
SARAH (*rising*). No, dear, it isn't the same thing, at all. (*She crosses to the armchair* L.C. *and sits on the* R. *arm.*) I could always kick up a row with the grocer until he gave me a good one to make up. I couldn't do that with Cedric.
HELEN (*despairingly*). Oh, heavens! Is there no reasoning with the woman? My poor girl, you must have something radically wrong with you, a complex or something. (*She crosses* L. *to the back of the armchair.*)
SARAH. I don't know about that; but I have felt lately that the women of our family seem fated to make a mess of things where marriage is concerned. Look at Mother.
HELEN (*moving to* L. *of the armchair*). What about her?
SARAH. Well, it's no use pretending that she and Father didn't fight like hell. What about Aunt Jessie and Uncle Ralph? Oh, and Aunt Zoe? Divorced three times.
HELEN. It shows she wasn't downhearted, anyway. (*She sits on the* L. *arm of the chair.*)
SARAH (*shaking her head*). No, dear, just carrying on the family tradition, as you and Roger did when your turn came!
HELEN. I suppose it doesn't occur to you that you're being very unfair to me!
SARAH. To you?
HELEN. Yes! What happened to Mother and Aunt Jessie and Aunt Zoe means nothing at all to you. You're determined to throw the whole responsibility for your ridiculous behaviour upon my experience with Roger.
SARAH (*earnestly*). Dearest—I don't want you to feel that!
HELEN. What happened to me is all over and done with; you've got your life to think of.
SARAH. I know—and I am thinking of it—very, very carefully.
HELEN. But—can't you see that if you love one another, then that's all that matters? (*Sentimentally.*) My dear Sarah, the love of a good man is——
SARAH (*cutting her short; rising and moving a little away from her to* C.). Worth more than rubies? Or is it the virtue of a good woman that somehow has to do with jewellery?
HELEN. Sarah, you really are——

(*The sound of the front-door bell is heard.* HELEN *starts violently and glares wildly round the room.*)

SARAH. That'll be Cedric, I expect.
HELEN (*rising and moving up* C.). Or—or Roger.

SARAH (*going to her; remorsefully*). Dearest, and I'd forgotten! Oh, why did you let me worry you with my stupid affairs, when——?
HELEN (*as* POYNTER *comes in from* R. *on the rostrum*). Ssh!
(POYNTER *crosses and goes off to* L. HELEN *crosses to the mirror as soon as he has disappeared.*)
Sarah—tell me quickly—have I changed much?—Much older?
SARAH (*soothingly, moving down to her*). No, darling, much more lovely.
HELEN (*agitatedly*). And—and, Sarah—they don't *all* turn yellow and go bald?
SARAH. No, darling, of course not——

(*She breaks off as* POYNTER *re-enters from* L., *followed by* CEDRIC NORREYS.)

POYNTER (*announcing*). Mr. Norreys, madam. (*He moves down to behind the table.*)
HELEN. Oh!——

(*The two women relax and move a little apart, as* CEDRIC *descends the two steps from the hall and advances towards them. He is thirty-five years of age, and looks slightly older; of medium height, and pleasing though quite unremarkable appearance. His clothes are extremely well-cut and betray a certain fastidious attention to detail. His speech is rather precise, and his manner, at any rate upon his entry, suggests a shy and rather self-effacing personality. His motor-coat is still folded over his arm.*)

SARAH (*going to* CEDRIC *and bringing him down stage—quickly recovering herself*). Cedric! Here you are, darling, at last. (*To* HELEN.) Helen, this is Cedric.
CEDRIC (C., *punctiliously*). How do you do? It's most kind of you to have me for the week-end, Mrs. Storer.
HELEN (*who has not entirely recovered her self-possession*). I'm so glad you were able to come. . . . Poynter, take Mr. Norreys' things.

(POYNTER *crosses down to* CEDRIC.)

SARAH (L. *of* CEDRIC, *indicating* POYNTER). No, dear, over there.

(CEDRIC *hands his hat and gloves to* POYNTER, *who has been hovering in the background.*)

And the coat, dear——
POYNTER. Thank you, sir.
HELEN. Mr. Norreys is in the West room, Poynter.
POYNTER. Yes, madam.

(*He goes off up* C. *to* L., *reappearing almost immediately with* CEDRIC'S *suitcase. Laden with this and the coat and hat, he crosses the rostrum and exits* R.)

ACT I.] LOVERS' LEAP. 15

HELEN. Would you like some tea, Mr. Norreys?
CEDRIC. Thank you, no; I lunched late in Winchester.
HELEN. A drink, then?
CEDRIC (*behind the settee*). Many thanks, but no.
SARAH. Did you have a nice time in Winchester? Did you get all emotional over the old school?
CEDRIC. Yes—very—at least, no—not at all!
SARAH. I always believe he had an affair with the matron.
CEDRIC. Oh! Sarah, really—how can you?
SARAH. All right, sweet, only my little joke, that's all. (*She goes to the table* R.C. *for a cigarette.*)
CEDRIC. Delightful country you have down here, Mrs. Storer.
HELEN (*crossing* R.). Yes, delightful—do sit down, won't you? (*She sits at* R. *end of the settee.*)

(SARAH *is at the table* R.C.)

(*After a short pause: polite conversation.*) Do you like the country, then, Mr. Norreys?
CEDRIC (*sitting* L. *on the settee*). I almost think I like it more than anything else. . . . I have a house in Scotland.
HELEN (*simulating intense interest*). Scotland! Oh, yes?
CEDRIC. The North of Scotland.
HELEN. Oh, the North of Scotland. (*After a short pause.*) Remote.
CEDRIC. I beg your pardon?
HELEN. Very remote, the North of Scotland.
CEDRIC. Oh, yes, very. (*Another short pause.*) But very beautiful, Mrs. Storer.
HELEN. I believe so. I'm always telling myself I must go there some time.
SARAH. Are you, dear? (*She moves down* L.C. *and sits in the armchair.*)

(*There is a rather long pause.*)

HELEN. Do smoke if you care to, Mr. Norreys.
CEDRIC (*after feeling in his pocket and discovering he has left his case in his overcoat*). Thank you—not just now.

(*Another pause. Then:*)

(*After racking his brains.*) The West Coast of Ireland, too, is very beautiful.
SARAH. Oh, Lord! They're off again! (*She puts one leg on the arm of her chair.*)
CEDRIC (*to* SARAH). I beg your pardon?
SARAH. Don't leave gallant little Wales out of this.
HELEN. Sarah, please.
SARAH (*rising and coming* R. *to above the settee*). I'm sorry, my dears; but I do want you to get to know each other; and, after

all, we're only here till Monday. Don't you think you could start right off by calling one another by your christian names? I always think that's such a help.

CEDRIC (*shyly*). Of course—I should like to very much if Mrs.——

SARAH. Helen——

CEDRIC. If—if Helen would allow me to.

HELEN. Oh, please do—Cedric.

SARAH (*coming to* L. *of the settee*). There! That's much more cosy! (*To* CEDRIC.) Now, tell me, have you noticed anything curious about your ears, this past half-hour or so?

CEDRIC (*touching one nervously*). No. Why, do they look curious?

SARAH. No more than usual. They haven't been burning?

CEDRIC. Not in the least.

SARAH (*sitting on the* L. *arm of the settee*). Then, they should have been, because I've been telling Helen about—us.

CEDRIC (*after a pause, embarrassed*). Oh—yes.

SARAH. And I may as well tell you, Cedric, that she's not a bit sympathetic.

HELEN. I find it difficult to be sympathetic about something which frankly I do not understand.

SARAH. Well, darling, I'm sure I've done my best to make you understand.

HELEN. You talked a great deal of rubbish, Sarah. (*To* CEDRIC.) The most I've been able to gather from it all is that you, Mr.—er—Cedric, are in love with my sister.

CEDRIC (*fervently*). I adore her!

HELEN. And that she is in love with you.

CEDRIC. Try as I may, I can't get used to the idea. It seems too fantastic to suppose that anything so wonderful could ever happen to me. I mean—why should she——

HELEN (*silencing him with a gesture*). We won't dwell upon that just now. We'll simply say that you're in love with one another; but you're not at all sure that you wish to marry.

CEDRIC (*quickly*). But I do! (*Then floundering, as he catches* SARAH'S *eye*.) At least—I mean——

HELEN. Well?

CEDRIC. I—that is, we—both wish to make reasonably sure that the—er—whichever course we adopt will be the one most calculated to lead to our ultimate happiness.

HELEN. Whichever course? Meaning by that, that my sister is to be either your wife or—or your mistress?

CEDRIC (*wincing at the last word*). Well—yes—I'm afraid that's what it amounts to.

HELEN. I see.

(*There is a pause.*)

CEDRIC. I wonder if I might change my mind and have a brandy and soda?

HELEN (*indicating the sideboard*). You'll find drinks in that cupboard.

CEDRIC. Thank you.

(SARAH *takes* CEDRIC *over behind the settee to the sideboard* R.)

SARAH (*coming down again to below* R. *end of settee*). Please understand, Helen, I will not allow you to bully Cedric. (*She sits on the stool at the desk.*)

HELEN. Bully him! I'd like to bash both your stupid heads together.

CEDRIC (*with a nervous laugh—squirting soda into his drink*). Oh, come!

HELEN. I would!

CEDRIC (*moving down to behind the settee with his drink*). I—I'm afraid you feel very strongly about this.

HELEN. How can I help it when I'm given quite clearly to understand that I'm responsible?

(*As* SARAH *starts to speak.*)

Be quiet, Sarah!

CEDRIC. You? Oh, but——

HELEN. Isn't it just because my own marriage was a failure, that this state of affairs between you two has come about?

(*As* SARAH *tries again to interrupt.*)

No, no, it's too late now for you to try to deny it.

CEDRIC (L. *of the settee*). I have been very sorry indeed to hear of your—er—unfortunate experience.

HELEN. About which you know nothing at all.

(CEDRIC *drinks.*)

You see, in our case there were *very* exceptional circumstances. (*She rises and crosses* L. *to the piano.*)

SARAH. Exceptional. Oh? (*She gives a little laugh.*)

HELEN. Yes, there were—and please don't laugh.

SARAH. I'm sorry, darling. But do tell us all about the exceptional circumstances—or is Cedric too young?

HELEN (*to* CEDRIC). Do sit down, won't you?

(CEDRIC *sits* L. *on the settee, placing his glass beside him on the arm of the settee.*)

You see—well—I suppose you'd call it a matter of temperament. His and mine.

CEDRIC. Were they so very—er——

B

HELEN. Yes, they were. They were opposed, utterly opposed.
CEDRIC. Such a pity.
HELEN. It was a great deal more than that; it was a tragedy.
(*She crosses to* L. *end of the settee.*)

(CEDRIC *moves his drink to* R. *seat of the settee.*)

CEDRIC. Oh, of course.
HELEN. You see, we loved one another, but that didn't stop us from getting on one another's nerves. We hated making one another miserable; but that didn't prevent us from doing it.
SARAH. It certainly did not! You quarrelled incessantly!
HELEN (C., *to her*). But never about anything that really mattered. (*To* CEDRIC.) Oh, it was all so silly! Childish! (*She moves to the table* R.C. *and helps herself to a cigarette.*) There's no denying, of course, that Roger *was* difficult.
SARAH. Difficult! If I repeated what you used to call him, Cedric would probably faint!
HELEN. Sarah, please! (*Moving to* R. *end of the settee.*) I'm trying to look at it all dispassionately, so that I may help you. . . . We'll say he had some irritating qualities. While I, of course, had my share.
SARAH. Nonsense, dear.
HELEN (*sitting* R. *on the settee*). Oh, but—yes, I was very silly.

(*As* HELEN *sits,* CEDRIC *moves his drink from the seat and places it on the* L. *arm again.*)

SARAH. You weren't any sillier than most women.
HELEN. No, perhaps not.
CEDRIC. I'm sure you were not nearly as silly as—— (*He lights his lighter for* HELEN.)
SARAH. Yes, dear?
CEDRIC. Nothing.
HELEN. Thunderstorms, for instance. (*Sighing.*) It's stupid of me, but the first rumble of thunder sends me scuttling in a panic to the boot-cupboard.
CEDRIC (*sympathetically*). I have an aunt who's just the same.
HELEN. Have you? I keep a bottle of sherry in there now, and a tin of Marie biscuits, on purpose. But my husband, though, could never understand my being scared, and he'd be all freezingly calm and just pour out statistics and things to prove I'd no right to be afraid. And the more he talked, the worse I'd get, until the whole thing would explode in a violent scene. (*Reminiscently.*) It was during one of our thunderstorm quarrels, I remember, that I bit his finger. (*She rises, and moves round* R. *to the back of the settee.*)
CEDRIC. Good gracious!
HELEN. Right through to the bone. (*She crosses down* L.)

CEDRIC (*clicking his tongue*). Tck! tck! tck!
HELEN. And then there was his Egyptology. (*She turns* R. *again.*)
CEDRIC. What did you do to that?
HELEN. His Egyptology?
CEDRIC. Oh—I beg your pardon.
HELEN. Every hour he spent poring over those dreadful drab books, or wandering round some dreary museum, I regarded as a deliberate insult to myself. (*Moving up and down at the back of the table* R.C.) I don't believe I'd have felt it half as much if he'd neglected me for another woman. But there was nothing to be done about Egypt. . . . And in the end, Egypt won.
CEDRIC. Really!
HELEN. For it was there he went when he left me. (*She sighs.*) He just walked out of the house one night, saying that he was going to take the dog for a walk. He left a note on the hall table, and the next I heard was a post card from Gibraltar.
CEDRIC. Tck! tck!
SARAH. A long walk to take a dog, Cedric.
HELEN. He wrote me a charming letter when he arrived in Egypt; and, of course, he's been most generous over money.
SARAH. That was the least he could do, considering the mess he'd made of your life.
HELEN (*sharply*). My life isn't a mess, Sarah.
CEDRIC (*tentatively*). Of course, you could have divorced him.
HELEN. And doesn't the fact that I haven't, prove I'm perfectly happy as I am . . . (*going to* L. *end of the settee*) and, at any rate, you do see, don't you?
SARAH. See? What does he see?
HELEN (*moving* L.). Why, that our experience was exceptional, and that for you to——
SARAH (*rising*). Exceptional, my foot! (*She moves round above the table* R.C. *to* C.)
HELEN (*down* L.C. *below the armchair*). Sarah!
SARAH (*coming down* C.). Oh, I don't expect it would be thunderstorms and Egyptology with us; Heaven knows there are more ways than one of sinking a ship. . . . Even now, I'm not entirely blind to the fact that Cedric has his share of irritating qualities.
CEDRIC (*rising*). Oh—but, my dear, you must tell me about them, and I'll—— (*He goes to* SARAH'S R.)
SARAH (*cutting him short*). Oh, but I don't mind them now—because, you see, I haven't the right to. But once I find myself securely married to you, I'll probably begin to think I have the right; and then—well—(*she concludes with an expressive gesture*) where are we?
HELEN. Oh, do stop talking rubbish!
SARAH (*with a little laugh, then very definitely, taking* CEDRIC'S *arm*). Now, Helen, Cedric and I are going to belong to one another.

That is definite. All we insist is, that we be allowed to choose whether we turn the key in the lock or leave the door off the latch.

(HELEN *is about to make a pretty vigorous retort; then, as though realizing the futility of any further argument, she shrugs her shoulders, and stubs her cigarette in the ashtray on the piano.*)

HELEN. Well, all I can say is—very well, then—that's that!
SARAH. I'm sorry, darling, but I'm afraid it is.
CEDRIC (*crossing to* HELEN). Of one thing I would like to assure you: whether Sarah and I marry, or whether we—er—don't, I promise you I shall never treat her as that scoundrel treated you.
HELEN. Roger was not a scoundrel.
CEDRIC. Not? A man who could walk out of the house and desert you as he did? He was a cad, and nothing would give me greater satisfaction than an opportunity to tell him so to his face. (*To* SARAH.) I mean it.

(*Door-bell. A loud ring.*)

SARAH. You little know, my dear, how very soon that opportunity is likely to occur.

(POYNTER *crosses the rostrum from* R. *and goes off to* L.)

CEDRIC. What do you mean?

(SARAH *nods her head significantly towards* HELEN.)

I say—is anything the matter?

(*The first note of the bell has startled* HELEN *into a little gasp. She is standing very tense and rigid, as though fighting down an impulse to fly from the room.* CEDRIC *stares at her bewilderedly.*)

SARAH (*her hand on his arm*). Come along, and let me show you your room. (*She takes* CEDRIC'S *arm and brings him up* R.C.)
CEDRIC (*still staring at* HELEN). But——
HELEN (L.). No—no—don't leave me, Sarah!

(SARAH *gives her a sharp look, then picks up* CEDRIC'S *half-finished drink from the settee, and hurries over to the sideboard for more brandy.*)

SARAH (*crossing and thrusting the glass into her hand*). Here—drink this!

(HELEN *lifts the glass to her lips and unthinkingly swallows half the contents at one gulp. The effect is instantaneous and devastating; a short spasm of gasping and choking, culminating in a violent hiccough.*)

HELEN. Oh, God! Look what you've done to me! Hic!

Act I.] LOVERS' LEAP. 21

SARAH (*hissing at her*). Pull yourself together! Courage!
(*A man's voice is heard off.* SARAH *darts back to* CEDRIC, *who is standing* R. *in a state of complete bewilderment.*)
CEDRIC. Look here——
SARAH. Ssh! (*She takes* CEDRIC *to* R. *end of the settee.*)

(POYNTER, *followed by* ROGER, *enters from* L.)

ROGER (*to* POYNTER, *who is about to announce him*). It's all right, don't bother.

(POYNTER *goes off to* R.)

(ROGER *is somewhere between thirty-five and forty, tall, bronzed, and quite attractive-looking. He is wearing a flannel suit, and is carrying his hat and gloves. He hesitates a second, as though dazzled by his sudden emergence from the sunlight of outside, then descends the two steps and advances towards* CEDRIC *and* SARAH. *He has not yet noticed* HELEN, *who is still down* L.)

SARAH (*as he approaches her*). No. (*Pointing to* HELEN.) Over there.
ROGER (*swinging round and seeing* HELEN). Oh, yes! Helen, my dear! (*He crosses* L. *to* HELEN.)

(HELEN, *momentarily incapable of speech, and still clutching the glass in her hand, stares at him stupidly. Then :*)

HELEN. Hic! (*She attempts to cover this with a little self-conscious cough.*)

(ROGER *has made an impulsive step towards her, but at this he pauses, disconcerted, then turns again to* SARAH.)

ROGER. And you're Sarah! Little Sarah! How are you?
SARAH (*above* R. *end of the settee, drawing herself up very formally*). Extremely well. This is Mr. Norreys. Cedric, this is Roger.
CEDRIC (R.C., *starting*). Who? (*Quickly recovering.*) I beg your pardon. (*He shakes hands with* ROGER.)
ROGER (C.). How do you do?
SARAH. And where is the dog?
ROGER. Dog? (*He whistles.*) I don't see any dog?—Oh, the dog!
SARAH. Oh!... (*To* CEDRIC.) Come along, Cedric.

(*She turns and goes hurriedly up the stairs, followed by* CEDRIC, *the latter casting a backward and still completely bewildered glance at* ROGER *as they go off. For a very short space,* ROGER *and* HELEN, *who has never taken her eyes off him from the moment of his entry, face each other across the room in silence. Then, placing his hat and gloves on the table, he crosses over to her.*)

ROGER (*with a little smile*). Well, Helen . . .
HELEN. Hic!
ROGER. Er—may I?

(*He takes the glass from her, sniffs it, and places it on the table* R.C. *There is a very short silence. Then :*)

HELEN (*down* L., *still staring at him fascinatedly*). But—you're not a bit yellow or bald.

ROGER (*coming down* C.). Good heavens! Did you expect I would be? . . . You haven't changed much, either, Helen. . . . I think perhaps it would be nice if we kissed, don't you?

(*She holds up her face to him.*)

HELEN (*just as his lips are nearing hers*). Hic!—I'm so sorry.

(*He draws back, frowning slightly, then :*)

ROGER (*moving a little away from her*). Hiccoughs. Most unpleasant. Entirely a matter of breath-control. No one need have them.

HELEN. As a matter of fact, I never do.—Hic!
ROGER. No, dear. Perhaps if you were to sit down.
HELEN. They say a cold key—— (*She sits in the armchair* L.C.)
ROGER. Old woman's drivel! You mind if I smoke? (*He crosses up to the table.*)
HELEN. Oh, do!

(*He takes a cigarette from the box on the table* R.C., *then moves to the* L. *end of the settee.*)

ROGER. I see you've had the room refurnished. (*He lights his cigarette.*)
HELEN. Soon after you left; I felt I had to do something. You like it?
ROGER. Very much. But then, you always had perfect taste in everything. I always thought that.
HELEN. You would, naturally.
ROGER. New pictures, too. Turned all my old family portraits out, I see, even Uncle Hubert.
HELEN. I've put him in the housemaid's bedroom.
ROGER. I say—well, really, I do think——
HELEN. From some of the stories I've heard of Uncle Hubert, he'll be thoroughly at home there.
ROGER (*sitting on the* L. *arm of the settee*). My letter would be a bit of a surprise, eh?
HELEN. A very big surprise, Roger.
ROGER. It was all done on the spur of the moment—my coming home from Egypt. There were one or two matters to be attended to . . . and so . . . here I am.
HELEN. Yes. . . . I'm finding it very difficult to realize.

ACT I.] LOVERS' LEAP. 23

ROGER. I know; I'm not finding it too easy myself.

HELEN (*speaking rapidly with a nervous animation*). I've so often pictured our meeting. I always imagined that it would all be intensely dramatic, and very, very—oh—you know. . . . And it isn't a bit, is it?—Hic!

ROGER. No, thank God! In any case, it would be difficult to be intensely dramatic through a gale of hiccoughs.

HELEN. Oh, I think they've gone now.

ROGER (*rising*). I'm glad. (*He crosses up to the table.*)

HELEN. Hic! Oh!

ROGER. Not quite. (*He turns and flicks his cigarette-ash into the ashtray.*)

(*There is a short, constrained pause. Then :*)

HELEN. Are you . . . staying long?

ROGER (*crossing down* R.). Well, I'd like to be in London fairly early this evening.

HELEN. No; in England, I was meaning.

ROGER. Oh, about a month.

HELEN. Only a month?

ROGER. Quite long enough, I imagine. (*He moves to* L. *end of the settee.*)

HELEN. Oh, of course, I expect you're aching all the time to get back to your Egyptology. How's it going, by the way?

ROGER. Going? Good heavens! You talk about it as though it were a patent medicine or something. (*He crosses, above the armchair, to* L.)

HELEN. I'm sorry.

ROGER (*stiffly*). As a matter of fact, if you really want to know, I may say I have no cause to feel despondent about my work. My reconstructed ground plan of the temple of Abydos was—er—very flatteringly received in certain quarters. And, of course, the Anatneferti tomb excavations last year. (*He crosses up* R.)

HELEN. Oh, yes, I read all about that in the " Graphic."

ROGER. Not really?

HELEN (*rising*). I felt so terribly proud to think that you were my—that I—that I knew you.

ROGER (*by the bookcase, obviously gratified*). That was nice of you, Helen. Very nice of you.

(*There is another short pause.*)

HELEN (*crossing* R. *and sitting* C. *of the settee*). And are you quite happy, Roger?

ROGER (*at the back of the settee*). Oh, yes, I suppose so. (*Then with a swift change of tone, moving to* L. *end of the settee.*) At least—no—not very.

HELEN (*looking up at him*). What?

ROGER. In fact, at times—I'm most damnably unhappy. (*He

moves up to the table.) I'm lonely, that's what it is—yes, I'm—I'm lonely, Helen. . . . Just lately, it's got so bad I knew I'd have to do something about it—(*coming down and standing by* L. *end of settee*) and so I decided I'd come to England and—and ask you.

HELEN. Ask me?

ROGER. Because—after all—it's in your hands, Helen.

HELEN. Mine?

ROGER. Yes. . . . Whether I'm to go on being lonely or not.

HELEN (*looking away from him, faintly*). Oh—I see.

(*The next instant he is sitting beside her,* L., *his right arm along the back of the settee.*)

ROGER. Helen—please—I want you to——

HELEN (*still more faintly*). Yes, Roger?

ROGER. I want you to be very kind to me and—and divorce me.

HELEN (*turning to him after a moment of stunned silence*). Divorce you!

ROGER. Yes.

HELEN. Oh, I see! . . .

ROGER. Good heavens!—you didn't think I was going to ask you to——? (*She does not speak.*) But what would be the use? We tried, both of us, that other time, and we failed—hopelessly —and you know it.

HELEN (*slowly*). Yes, I suppose we did. It wasn't because I didn't love you, Roger. I did—terribly.

ROGER. And I you, my dear. During those few months we lived together, I worshipped the very ground you walked on . . . excepting on those occasions when I prayed to God it might open and swallow you up.

HELEN. Roger!

ROGER (*holding up his forefinger—significantly*). Look!

HELEN (*glancing at it, then quickly away*). Oh—that!

ROGER (*waggling it at her*). Yes, that! When folk out there ask what it is, I tell 'em it's a snake-bite.

HELEN (*moving away a little, on the settee*). I think you might have invented a prettier explanation.

ROGER. Well, it wouldn't have been any prettier to call it a wife-bite! No, Helen, it's no use.

HELEN. No use?

ROGER. I'm terribly sorry, but there it is. (*He rises and goes round* L. *of the settee to the back.*)

HELEN (*getting up—sharply*). Just one moment. Are you under the impression I'm trying to lure you back to me? I suppose you mean by that, I'm the sort of woman these days who could never attract anybody—is that so? (*She is standing by* R. *end of the settee.*) Just a rag and a bone and a hank of hair that no man would look at twice. I see. (*She crosses to the armchair* L.C.)

ROGER (*above* R. *end of the settee*). Nonsense. You're a very charming woman still.
HELEN (*turning*). How very like you to add that " still."
ROGER. I mean it; you are a very charming woman.
HELEN. Eh?
ROGER (*with a little smile*). Full stop, my dear.
HELEN. Thank you. (*Moving to the piano.*) After all, we did love one another, didn't we?
ROGER. Madly! Oh, quite madly!
HELEN. Then——
ROGER. I believe its far from unusual for two people to love one another and lead a cat-and-dog life at one and the same time. (*He crosses up* C.)
HELEN. That's right, go on. Rob me of the one comforting thought that my experience was unique!
ROGER (*moving down* C.). I prefer to find my comfort in the knowledge that I had the sense to know when I'd had enough of a bad thing.
HELEN. Well—of all the—— (*With an obvious effort she checks a vigorous retort.*)

(*After a moment, he continues:*)

ROGER. And, after all, my dear Helen, I wasn't only thinking of myself when I did what I did. It was for your peace of mind as well as my own. I believe I said something of the sort in the letter I left behind.
HELEN. Did you? I forget.
ROGER. You know, I've often wondered just what you did that night—after you'd found my note on the hall table and realized. (*He sits on the* L. *arm of the settee.*)
HELEN (*at the back of the armchair* L.C.). I played all the military band records we had in the house, one after another, at top speed, then took a couple of aspirins and went to bed.
ROGER (*blankly*). Oh—you did!
HELEN. I suppose you always pictured me screaming, wailing and tearing my hair out in fistfuls. I'm sorry to disillusion you.
ROGER. As if I minded one way or another.
HELEN. Now I come to think of it, though, I believe I did cry a little the next morning.
ROGER. Ah!
HELEN. I was terribly fond of that dog.
ROGER (*stung to sudden fury; jumping up and advancing towards her*). Now, look here, Helen, I've not come all this way to listen to you——

(*At that moment* SARAH'S *and* CEDRIC'S *voices are heard.* HELEN *immediately whisks a large full-blown rose from the bowl on the piano and trips towards him with it, meeting him as he advances towards her.*)

HELEN. There, that looks so sweet.
ROGER (*taken aback by this sudden manœuvre*). Here, what on earth are you doing?
    (SARAH *and* CEDRIC *appear on the rostrum from* R.)
HELEN (*very sotto voce, thrusting the rose into his buttonhole, as they appear*). Ssh! Quiet! (*In a louder voice.*) There, my dear, that looks so sweet! (*Pretending to become aware of the other two —brightly.*) Ah, there you are, then!
SARAH (*up* C.). I'm just going to show Cedric the garden. He adores gardens.
HELEN. Do, dear, do; and don't forget to look at the orange-blossom, it's so lovely this year.
SARAH. We will, dear. We'll have a look at the love-lies-bleeding, too. (*To* CEDRIC.) Come along, darling.
    (*They go off to* L.)
HELEN (*with a sigh of relief*). That's what I call presence of mind! (*She crosses to* R.C.)
ROGER. A pity you couldn't manage it without making me look like a Harvest Festival. (*Taking the rose from his buttonhole and handing it to her.*) Here, take it.
HELEN (*taking it from him*). Thank you. (*She crosses to the piano.*)
ROGER (C.). And supposing we avoid the risk of any further tomfoolery by getting to business at once.
HELEN (*poking the rose back among the others in the bowl*). Yes, dear, of course.
ROGER. Very well, then, what about it?
HELEN (*starting at his tone*). What about what?
ROGER (*with the elaborate calm of one who is straining every nerve to control himself*). A few minutes ago, I believe I mentioned the question of divorce.
HELEN. Of course you did. I hadn't forgotten.
ROGER (*much louder*). Well? Will you or won't you?
HELEN. Roger! Really! What a way in which to ask!
ROGER (*forcing a calmer tone*). As I've already explained, I should like to be in London fairly early this evening, and——
HELEN. And you'd like some tea at once! Of course. (*She starts to hurry towards the bell-push,* R.)
ROGER. No! No!
    (*She pauses and looks at him inquiringly.*)
Please.
    (*She returns to him more slowly.*)
Thank you.
(*They are facing each other, he with his hands clasped behind his back.*)
Now, seriously, don't you think it's about time something was

Act I.] LOVERS' LEAP. 27

done about it—us, I mean? I think it's our positive duty to—well—take steps of some sort.

HELEN. What sort?

ROGER (c.). Divorce. . . . It would be perfectly easy to arrange: grounds of desertion, etc., naturally.

HELEN (R.C.). I see.

ROGER. All quite straightforward and no unpleasantness for you, I promise.

HELEN. I shouldn't have the King's Proctor nosing about here disguised as a scullery-maid? I couldn't bear it.

ROGER. Certainly not! After all, I did desert you.

HELEN (*coming down a little*). You did, indeed.

ROGER (*following her down*). Yes, well. . . . To-morrow at the latest you can set the wheels in motion by writing me a letter imploring me to return to you.

HELEN. Imploring? Ho!

ROGER. Asking, then, if the word is more agreeable. Remind me before I leave, and I'll give you a stamped addressed envelope.

HELEN. Oh—thank you.

ROGER. Not at all. . . . Having received your letter, I shall at once reply to the effect that nothing on earth would induce me ever to live with you again.

HELEN. But is there any point in my writing a letter to which I already know the answer?

ROGER. My dear Helen, it's the merest formality.

HELEN. I see. (*She crosses to above the settee.*)

ROGER. Well, after that, there's nothing left for you to do but to visit your lawyer and let matters take their course. As regards money, I'm not a poor man, as you know, and I shall continue to be as generous to you as you could wish. In fact, Helen, it's my intention to show you every possible consideration.

HELEN. You'd better not overdo it, or I might find myself quite unable to part with you at the last moment.

ROGER (L.C., *ignoring this and glancing at his wrist-watch*). Now—are there any questions you'd like to ask me before I leave?

HELEN (*coming* c.). Yes. One.

ROGER. Well?

HELEN. What's her name?

ROGER (*above the armchair* L.C.). I beg your pardon?

HELEN (*crossing below the armchair to the piano*). Her name, Roger . . . because, of course, you are going to marry again, aren't you?

ROGER. I never said so.

HELEN. You've had a grand time these past seven years, rooting among the private affairs of people who've been dust for centuries——

(*As he starts to interrupt.*)

Be quiet! I'm speaking. For all you cared, the state of affairs could have gone on for ever, so long as *you* were free to do all the things *you* wanted to do, in the place in which *you* most wanted to do them. In fact, you were well on the way to forgetting my existence entirely, if something hadn't cropped up in your precious scheme of life to remind you of it. What that something is it doesn't need a super-brain to guess. Ha! (*She turns away from him very deliberately and moves to down* L., *below the piano.*)

ROGER (*with a little shrug and speaking in very level tones*). Age has not increased your self-control, I'm sorry to notice.

HELEN (*turning on him*). Oh, stop being superior, damn you!

(ROGER *snatches his gloves from the table* R.C., *and starts to struggle into them.*)

And why are you doing that?

ROGER. Once bitten, twice shy, my dear.

(HELEN *takes a book from the piano and is about to throw it at him.* ROGER, *behind the settee, takes up a cushion to defend himself. After a moment they both relax.*)

(*Putting his gloves in his pocket.*) Helen, let's try not to quarrel for the space of five whole minutes. Now, come and sit down.

(HELEN *hesitates, then crosses* R. *and sits* L. *on the settee.* ROGER *sits* R. *on the settee.*)

There! (*A pause of a second or two.*) Now—as to the possibility of my re-marrying, it's true that I have—er—some such project in mind.

HELEN. Of course you have. Tell me her name at once.

ROGER (*rather impressively*). Lady Emily Willock.

HELEN (*the name clearly meaning nothing to her*). Lady Emily Willock. And who might she be?

ROGER. You've never heard of Lady Emily Willock?

HELEN (*shaking her head*). Is she as notorious as all that?

ROGER. "Celebrated" is the word I should use. As an Egyptologist she has no equal among her own sex, and precious few among the men.

HELEN. What? You mean to tell me she's an Egyptologist too?

ROGER (*nodding*). Yes, certainly.

HELEN. I'd no idea that women went in for it.

ROGER. I do wish, Helen, you would not speak of Egyptology as though it were one of the more curious vices.

HELEN. Where did you meet her?

ROGER. Well, if you must know, our first meeting took place no more than six weeks ago, in the tomb of Rameses III.

HELEN. A cheery beginning! Go on, tell me what you said to one another.

ROGER. So far as I remember, I said, "Lady Emily Willock, I

believe?" And the next thing I realized was that it was two hours later.

HELEN. You mean she'd knocked you unconscious or something?

ROGER. I mean, our conversation was so absorbing that time just ceased to exist.

HELEN. Go on, tell me what happened next?

ROGER. And with our mutual interest, it was only natural that we should arrange to meet again.

HELEN. And again and again and again. Go on.

ROGER. I wish you'd stop saying "go on." In any case, there's nothing more to tell.

HELEN. But—you've asked her to marry you?

ROGER. Certainly not. Under the present circumstances, that would have been the action of a cad.

HELEN. Oh——

ROGER. It's true, on the night before leaving for England, I did go so far as to hint that I might, in the not too distant future, be able to suggest a more permanent relationship for the two of us; and she in turn conveyed the impression that there would be no objections on her part.

HELEN. Good old Emily!

(*He winces.*)

And are you terribly in love with her, Roger?

ROGER. In love? Good God, no! What an idea!

HELEN (*blankly*). Oh——

ROGER. Of course, I'm strongly attracted to her, but not in that way.... (*Rising.*) Believe me, Helen, I was not exaggerating when I told you I was lonely. (*Going up to behind the settee.*) Curious moods and yearnings would come over me at odd moments —especially in the evenings.

HELEN. Horrid for you.

ROGER. And then one day, almost as you might say in a flash, I knew.

HELEN. Ah!

ROGER. What I needed was companionship, someone whose interests were my interests, someone who—oh, but you know what I mean!

HELEN. And at that critical moment—up pops Emily. (*She rises.*) I see. (*She moves to the table and helps herself to a cigarette. She proceeds, very unhurriedly, to light her cigarette, then, mechanically, as though lost in thought, she drops the match into the ashtray. Murmuring to herself.*) Emily . . .

ROGER. What?

HELEN (*at the back of the settee*). Would she make you very happy, Roger?

ROGER. Yes, I think she would.

HELEN. Succeed where I failed.
ROGER (R. *of* HELEN, *generously*). My dear Helen, we both of us failed. We had an infinite capacity for loving one another, but none whatever for making one another happy.
HELEN. Very sad.
ROGER. Very. (*Cheerfully*.) Still, no use crying over spilt milk. Can you lend me an envelope?
HELEN. What?—Oh, yes, you'll find plenty in the writing-desk.

(ROGER *goes* R. *to the desk, sits before it, takes an envelope and proceeds to write. She wanders to down* L. CEDRIC *and* SARAH'S *voices are heard, and, after a moment, they appear on the rostrum from* L. SARAH *first, her arms laden with flowering branches of syringa, in this country frequently called orange-blossom*.)

SARAH (*coming down* L.C.—*to* HELEN). Darling, you were quite right; the orange-blossom *is* divine. (*She crosses* R.)
CEDRIC (*following*). Your garden is perfect, Mrs.—Helen.
HELEN. I'm so glad you like it.
SARAH (*suddenly noticing* ROGER *at the desk*). Oh—you still here?
ROGER. As you see. I'm afraid, Helen, I shall have to trespass on you for a stamp too.
HELEN. There's a book in one of the little pigeon-holes.
SARAH (*with dismay, looking at her flowers which are dropping*). Oh, look what's happened.
CEDRIC (*coming to her*). What is it? A caterpillar?
SARAH. The petals are falling!

(CEDRIC *picks up the petals at* SARAH'S *feet*.)

ROGER (*sticking a stamp on the envelope and thumping it with his fist*). Why, of course.
SARAH. Why "of course"? Do all flowers die at the sight of you?
ROGER. If you knew anything at all about such things, you'd know that that particular species, *Philadelphus Coronarius* is its name, invariably withers when gathered. (*He rises*.) It doesn't last.
SARAH. Aaah! You hear that, Cedric? It doesn't last! There's an omen for us, if you like.

(CEDRIC *laughs rather uncertainly*.)

HELEN (*sharply*). Sarah, don't be silly.
SARAH. What am I to do with them, anyway?
HELEN (*starting to cross* R.). I'll ring for Poynter to——
SARAH. No, no, don't bother; we'll find him and give them to him. (*To* CEDRIC.) Come along, darling.
CEDRIC (*as they turn to go out*). Let me carry them for you.
SARAH. Really, my dear, I'm quite capable of . . .

(*He is trying to take them from her, and she is refusing to allow him to, as they go up to the rostrum and off to* R. HELEN *moves up* L.)

ROGER (*crossing up to* HELEN). Is that sister of yours going to marry that man?

HELEN. I don't know—I—— (*Then with sudden, almost fierce determination, looking after them.*) Yes, she *is* going to marry him! She *is*!

ROGER (*raising his eyebrows slightly at her tone*). All right. You needn't snap my head off. (*Holding out the envelope.*) Here you are. I shall be staying at my club, as you see. I might as well make a little use of it, after all these years.

(*But* HELEN *is not paying any attention to him. After no more than a glance at the envelope, her gaze returns towards the entrance* R., *as though her thoughts are at the moment occupied by* CEDRIC *and* SARAH, *to the exclusion of all else.*)

(*In a louder tone.*) You might perhaps write the letter after dinner to-night, Helen. (*As she pays no attention.*) Helen——

HELEN (*turning to him, with the air of one who has come to a great decision*). Will you please ring that bell?

ROGER. Bell? Oh—— (*He goes* R. *and presses the bell, then moves a few paces down, then above the settee to* C. *again.*) I'm really not sure that I have time to stay to tea. . . . However, I can rely, can't I, on that letter reaching me in London by the first post on Monday morning?

HELEN (*up* L.C.). No, Roger, I'm afraid you can't.

ROGER. But——

(POYNTER *appears on the rostrum from* R.)

HELEN. Because you won't be in London on Monday morning.

ROGER. What?

POYNTER. You rang, madam?

HELEN (*to* ROGER). Is your car outside?

ROGER. Yes. Why?

HELEN (*to* POYNTER). Poynter, have it taken round to the garage, the luggage unstrapped and taken up to the East bedroom.

(*As* ROGER *utters an exclamation.*)

At once, Poynter!

POYNTER. Very good, madam.

(*He goes off to* L.)

ROGER (*to* HELEN, *explosively*). Look here—is that my luggage you've told him to take to the East bedroom?

HELEN. It is.

ROGER (*with forced calm*). May I ask why?

HELEN (*crossing him to the table* R.C.). Because that is the room where you'll be sleeping to-night.
ROGER (*turning*, C.). Ho! really—is it, indeed? We'll soon see about that! (*He turns swiftly to go up stage.*)
HELEN (*quickly*). Where are you going?
ROGER. To tell that fellow he's to do none of the things you told him to do, of course.
HELEN. In that case—— (*She tears the envelope across and across and tosses the bits on to the table.*)
ROGER (*arrested*). Oh! What does that mean?
HELEN (*very definitely*). It means, Roger, that if you want this divorce, you've got to earn it. (*She moves above the table to down* R.)
ROGER (*quite shrilly*). By allowing myself to be kidnapped into spending to-night in this house with you?
HELEN. Several nights, and several days.
ROGER. Sev——
HELEN. During which time your attitude to me will be entirely that of a loving and devoted husband.

(ROGER *is speechless.*)

(*Adding hastily.*) In the daytime only, of course. Alone in your East bedroom at night you'll be free to be just your own natural self.
ROGER. Will you stop talking nonsense and——

(*At that moment* POYNTER *enters on the rostrum from* L., *a large suitcase in each hand. He comes into the room and makes for the stairs.*)

HELEN. Of course, while you're being charming to me, I shall be equally charming to you.
ROGER (*crossing down* L.). I don't know what you're talking about, and I don't believe you do yourself. (*He turns and sees* POYNTER.) Hey! You! Take those back at once and strap them on again.
HELEN. You mean—you're really going?
ROGER (*crossing to* R.C.). I am! (*He picks up his hat.*)
HELEN (*in a fairly audible undertone*). Poor old Emily.
ROGER (*coming down to her*). What?

(POYNTER *comes back down the stairs.*)

HELEN (*holding out her hand to him and speaking in gushing hostess tones*). Good-bye, then. So glad to have seen you, sorry you can't stay. Some other time, perhaps. (*To* POYNTER, *whose compliance with* ROGER'S *command has been somewhat retarded by the difficulties of making a right-about turn when burdened with two heavy cases.*) Hurry, Poynter.
ROGER (*up* C., *shouting to* POYNTER, *just as the latter is going off to* L.). Here, wait a moment! (*Turning to* HELEN.) Now——

Helen (r.c.). Well? ...
Roger (*to* Poynter). Oh—put those things down.
Helen. Leave them there, Poynter. I'll ring for you presently.

(Poynter *puts the luggage down just* l. *of the stairs and goes off to* r.)

Roger (*as soon as he has gone*). Now—what did you mean by " Poor old Emily "?
Helen (*with a tiny shrug*). Just a sudden rush of feminine sympathy for another woman whose hopes are about to crash.
Roger. Crash? (*Moving to her* l.) Am I seriously to understand that unless I stay here, you refuse to divorce me?
Helen. You are, Roger.
Roger. Good God!
Helen. And, after all, I don't think I'm asking much; a matter of a few days, and the country's very nice at this time of year.
Roger (*putting his hat down on the table again*). What's your game? What are you going to get out of this?
Helen (*acidly*). Nothing at all, except possibly a few weeks in a Home through the strain of being polite to you. The person I'm hoping will benefit is Sarah. (*She crosses him to below the armchair* l.c.)
Roger (*following to* c.). Sarah? What's she going to get out of it?
Helen. A husband, I hope.
Roger. Oh! How?
Helen. She and the man you met just now are irresistibly attracted to one another.
Roger. Really? (*Crossing* r., *below the settee*.) Ah, well, I suppose Nature knows best.
Helen. There's only one thing that stops them rushing to a church.
Roger (r.). Some people have all the luck; nothing stopped us.
Helen (*tartly*). You're apparently all eagerness to try again, nevertheless.
Roger. Never mind about that. Tell me what's stopping them.
Helen. Our marriage.
Roger. Our mar——!
Helen (*crossing to* r.c., *below the settee*). They choose to look upon us as a warning.

(*He bursts into a loud laugh.*)

(*She turns on him furiously.*) I'm glad it amuses you to know that if they make a mess of their lives, it will be entirely due to us.
Roger (*checking his laughter*). Sorry. Go on.
Helen (*sitting at* l. *end of the settee*). Now, listen. The merest

hint of a divorce between you and me would be enough to send them careering off to Paris.

ROGER (*at* R. *end of the settee*). Then, don't tell them about the divorce; keep it dark.

HELEN (*kneeling up on the settee*). But don't you see that won't be enough? No. During this week-end, you and I have got to be a constant reminder of the beauty, sanctity and success of marriage.

ROGER (*down stage* R.). My God!

HELEN (*rising and going* R. *to him*). Be quiet and listen to me. (*Speaking rapidly and very earnestly.*) Now, our marriage, years ago, was a colossal mistake. To-day you came back to me, and within five minutes we were in one another's arms——

ROGER. What?

HELEN. Hold your tongue! In one another's arms. Do you understand?

ROGER (*after a pause, staring at her*). And you're seriously proposing that I shall take part with you in this damn silly charade?

HELEN. Well, I can't be a devoted couple all on my own, can I?

ROGER (*moving up* C., *round* R. *end of settee*). I never heard of anything so preposterous! Never! (*He moves down* L.)

HELEN (*complacently*). I don't agree. I think it's rather brilliant. It just sort of flashed across me.

ROGER (L.C.). It's the sort of thing that would flash across you.

HELEN. Oh!

ROGER (*pacing up and down*, C.). Here I come all these miles for the express purpose of offering you your freedom—and you try to make it the occasion for a nauseatingly silly practical joke.

HELEN. It is not a joke; I'm serious.

ROGER (*facing her*, C.). But—but, great heavens! Even if I consented, do you imagine they'd be deceived for one moment?

HELEN. It would be up to us to be so convincing that they will be.

ROGER. That's all very well, but if I stay one night under this roof, bang goes our divorce.

HELEN. Oh, of course, if it's too much trouble for you to pretend to be nice to me for a day or two, I'd better ring at once for your things to be put back into your car. (*She starts to move up* R.)

ROGER (*hurrying after her*). No, Helen, wait! Please.

(HELEN *turns, and there is a pause.*)

HELEN. Well?

ROGER (*above table* R.C.). You—you're so impulsive!—I can't just go off to London and leave matters in this state. I—I *must* know where I stand.

HELEN (*very directly*). *You* want me to do something for you and I want you to do something for me. (*With a gesture.*) That's where we *both* stand, my dear. (*On the last word, with the air of one who has said all there is to say on the subject, she turns and goes resolutely upstairs.*)

ROGER. Here! Where are you going?

HELEN. Mind your own business!

(*She proceeds on her way upstairs, and off.* ROGER *makes as if to follow her, then halts, defeated, shoulders hunched, hands thrust into trouser pockets, scowling after her. After a moment he jerks himself out of this attitude, strides over to* R. *and gives a vicious jab at the bell-push. Moving to the table* R.C., *he snatches up his hat and gloves, stands for a second or two, irresolute, then with a smothered exclamation tosses them back on to the table and moves down to beside the settee.* POYNTER *enters on the rostrum from* R.)

POYNTER. You rang, sir?

ROGER (*jerking his head in the direction of his luggage*). The East bedroom.

(POYNTER *picks up the luggage and goes out* R. *on the rostrum.* ROGER *is staring morosely in front of him as*

The CURTAIN *falls.*

ACT II

Scene 1

*It is about half-past eight in the evening of the same day.
Roger's photograph is now displayed upon the writing-desk.*

When the Curtain *rises,* Poynter *is moving unhurriedly about the room, emptying the ashtrays on to a salver. He is down* l. *by the piano, when* Cedric, *wearing a dinner-suit, comes in downstairs. After a glance towards* Poynter, *he goes to the bookcase up* r., *bending forward and peering rather shortsightedly at the titles.* Poynter, *his task finished, turns as if to go out.*

Poynter. Is there anything I can get you, sir ?
Cedric. No, thank you. At least——
Poynter. Yes, sir ?
Cedric. I suppose there isn't such a thing in the house as an " Encyclopædia Britannica " ?
Poynter. Oh, yes, sir. In the library.
Cedric (*unfamiliar with the geography of the house*). Library ? Oh——
Poynter. Allow me to get it for you, sir. (*He places the salver on the table* r.c. *and crosses to* r.) Did you require the entire " Encyclopædia," sir ?
Cedric. Oh, only one volume : the—the L one, if you please.
Poynter. The L, sir. Yes, sir.

(Poynter *goes off* r. Cedric *crosses* l., *behind the armchair, takes out his cigarette-case, puts it back, hums a little tune, breaking off with a cough as* Poynter *re-enters.*)

Poynter (*crossing* c. *and handing the volume*). This will be the volume, I believe, sir.
Cedric (*tucking it under his arm*). Oh, thank you, thank you very much indeed.

(Poynter *moves to the back of the table, takes up the salver, proceeds upstairs and goes off to* r. *While* Poynter *is in the room,* Cedric *remains standing* c. ; *the moment he is alone, he hurries over to the settee, sits, whisks the volume from under his arm, and commences to hunt with feverish haste through its pages. So absorbed is he, he is quite unaware of* Sarah *when, a moment later, she comes quietly downstairs. She is wearing a very beautiful and very sophisticated-looking evening gown. For a moment she stands look-*

ing at him, smiling a little; then she coughs. CEDRIC *starts, looks up, closes the book with a loud snap, rises and puts the book behind him.*)

SARAH (*coming down* C.). There's just one thing I do like about your face, Cedric, and that is that it's most expressive.

CEDRIC (*below the settee, with a little forced laugh*). Oh—I'm glad you like it for that!

SARAH. Yes, it tells me I've discovered you reading the sort of book you'd infinitely prefer not to be discovered reading.

CEDRIC (*hastily*). No, really, I——

SARAH (*at* L. *end of the settee*). Now, now, come, come. Tell me its title at once.

CEDRIC (*rather diffidently*). Well—if you must know—it was the "Encyclopædia Britannica."

SARAH. The—what, dear?

CEDRIC. The "Encyclopædia Britannica." (*Displaying it to her.*) You see?

SARAH. I do, dear; I do. And may I ask why?

CEDRIC (*with increased diffidence*). Well . . . there was something about which I—er—wanted a little information.

SARAH. Oh? Yes. What?

CEDRIC. Licences, in fact.

SARAH. Dog, gun, motor or marriage?

CEDRIC. Marriage, Sarah. . . . The—er—the special kind, you know; the sort you have when you don't want to waste any time.

SARAH (*looking at him*). Oh!

CEDRIC (*airily*). I just wondered how people who went in for that sort of thing set about getting them—and I thought the "Encyclopædia" might say something.

SARAH. And does it?

CEDRIC. I hadn't time to find out.

SARAH. Well, don't bother now. Come and sit down. (*She sits* L. *on the settee.*)

(*He puts the "Encyclopædia"* R. *on the settee, then sits beside her* R.)

CEDRIC (*after a moment, gazing at her*). You're—you're looking almost unbelievably beautiful to-night, Sarah.

SARAH. Am I, darling? Then why don't you kiss me?

CEDRIC. Oh—may I?

SARAH. You may.

(*He leans towards her, places his arm round her and kisses her. Just as the embrace seems on the verge of becoming quite passionate, he releases her, as though suddenly rather overwhelmed by his own boldness. She smiles.*)

CEDRIC. You know, Sarah . . . there's always one thing that—that spoils it when I'm kissing you.

SARAH. Oh!

CEDRIC. It never seems quite real; it's all too wonderful.
SARAH (*touching his cheek lightly*). Sweet.
CEDRIC. I suppose it's because nothing quite like it has ever happened to me before.
SARAH. That's *not* so good.
CEDRIC (*after a pause—continuing with difficulty*). I—I've had such a funny kind of life, Sarah.
SARAH. If this is leading up to a confession of a dirty past, don't you think you'd better wait until after dinner?
CEDRIC (*with a slight laugh*). I've nothing to confess, not a thing. That's just it.
SARAH. Just what?
CEDRIC. I mean—it just shows how empty life has been right up to the moment when I met you. (*Sighing.*) A desert waste, Sarah, until you came into my life and taught me its true meaning.
SARAH. You make me feel a little like a missionary, dear.
CEDRIC (*continuing*). Born rich, I didn't have to work; of a somewhat reserved disposition, I made few or no friends; games never appealed to me, and every hobby bored me stiff within a week. (*Sighing again.*) How simple life must be for those who, by hitting a little ball into a little hole, can be made to feel that they haven't lived their lives in vain.
SARAH. But aren't you taking yourself a wee bit too seriously?
CEDRIC (*gravely—shaking his head*). No; in moments such as this, when a man feels that his whole outlook has been revolutionized, I doubt if he can be too serious. . . .
SARAH. No, I suppose not.
CEDRIC. If only I could make you understand what you've done to me, Sarah.
SARAH. Let's take it for granted, shall we? And get me a cigarette, will you?
CEDRIC. How you've made everything seem different somehow. More thrilling, more real! How you've given me an interest, a purpose, something to live for.
SARAH. Have I done all that to you?
CEDRIC. And more.
SARAH. How lovely! The cigarettes are behind you, dear, on the table.
CEDRIC. Many a man, situated as I am, would have——
SARAH (*much louder*). Cigarettes, Cedric!
CEDRIC (*starting*). Oh—sorry! (*He rises and gets the box from the table* R.C., *and offers it to her.*)—would have gone to the dogs, through sheer boredom.
SARAH (*taking a cigarette*). I do so often wonder what those poor dogs can have done to deserve it.

(*He puts the box back on the table, then moves round* R. *end of settee.*)
And a match, please.

CEDRIC (*getting a lighter from his pocket*). So you see, don't you, that whatever happens—— (*He lights her cigarette.*)

SARAH. Thank you, darling.

CEDRIC (*kneeling on the settee beside her—very earnestly*). You do see, Sarah, that having found you, I'm determined never to let you go again—never!

SARAH. My dear, you're so fierce; you quite frighten me.

CEDRIC. We *are* always going to be together, aren't we? . . . We must be.

SARAH (*lightly, puffing at her cigarette*). Always, of course.

CEDRIC. Please say that again.

SARAH. Always.

CEDRIC (*leaning back, closing his eyes in quite an ecstasy*). How wonderful it sounds!

SARAH. Always. Always. Always. There!

CEDRIC (*sighing happily*). Marvellous!

SARAH (*leaning back*). Tell me, Cedric, this sudden interest of yours in marriage licences—doesn't mean that you've already made up your mind, does it?

CEDRIC (*sitting* R. *on the settee*). Certainly not. I should never dream of making up my mind until you had made up yours.

SARAH (*after a pause, during which she gazes at him*). When you say things like that, my dear, it makes me wonder whether you're almost too good to be true.

CEDRIC. I mean—we must both make up our minds together . . . and there's no harm in finding out about special licences beforehand —er—just in case, you know. (*As she does not speak.*) I said just in case, Sarah. (*He rises, crosses* L., *and puts the book on the armchair* L.C.)

SARAH. Yes, dear, I heard you.

CEDRIC. Now, look at Helen and Roger.

SARAH. What about them?

CEDRIC (*not looking at her*). As I looked out of my window, before dressing, I could see them both standing by the fishpond.

SARAH. Were they?

CEDRIC (*nodding—still not looking at her*). The setting sun was in my eyes, but I could almost swear her head was resting on his shoulder.

SARAH. Good heavens!

CEDRIC. The sight of them there struck me as curiously touching.

SARAH. I can remember when the sight of them standing by a pond would merely have made me wonder which would be pushed in first.

CEDRIC (*going to the table for a cigarette*). I know. But that's all over and done with now, forgotten . . . and under the circumstances, it's perhaps a little unkind to refer to it.

SARAH. Do you believe it's going to last, then, this reunion?

CEDRIC (*behind the settee*). My dear Sarah, I should be the most loathsome of cynics to doubt it. I'm not a particularly emotional man, but I'm not ashamed to admit that several times during tea, I had a decided lump in my throat.

SARAH. How uncomfortable for you, dear.

CEDRIC. To see them sitting there, passing one another the bread and butter, as though nothing in the world mattered now that they were together again . . . Little things, too, like her remembering that he took two lumps of sugar in his tea. Didn't that strike you as rather lovely?

SARAH. No, dear, no. I happen to know that he never took any. (*She puts her legs up on the settee.*)

CEDRIC. Anyhow, I shall always regard their experience as an example by which a great many husbands and wives might profit.

SARAH. Oh! You think it would be a good thing for them to fight like hell for eight months, live apart for seven years, then come together again?

CEDRIC (*moving down* R.). Certainly not. I'm afraid you wilfully misunderstand me, Sarah.

SARAH (*rising, crossing* L. *and putting her cigarette in the ashtray on the piano*). I'm sorry . . . but I don't think I quite like you, Cedric, when you're mushy.

CEDRIC. I'm not mushy. My feelings happen to have been deeply moved, that's all. . . . And if I may say so, I'm just a bit surprised at your own lack of enthusiasm.

SARAH. Darling, as soon as I'm quite convinced there's something to be glad about, then I promise you I'll ooze enthusiasm from every pore.

CEDRIC. Convinced? But, great heavens, you surely don't doubt——

SARAH. As soon as I'm convinced, Cedric.

CEDRIC (*breaking off and shrugging his shoulders*). Oh, well, perhaps we'd better talk about something else.

SARAH. Yes, dear.

CEDRIC. Let's talk about us.

(SARAH *goes to the piano and strikes three chords.*)

SARAH (*playing the opening bars of the "Wedding March" very softly as she speaks*). I think you told me a little untruth just now, when you said you hadn't made up your mind. You have, Cedric, haven't you?

CEDRIC (*in a louder tone*). No, I have not! I know what I want; but I also know it will be you who'll eventually make up my mind as to what I'm to have.

SARAH. Sounds a little involved, dear.

CEDRIC (*crossing to* R. *of the piano*). If you'll stop playing, I'll express myself more clearly.

SARAH (*ceasing to play*). Oh—I thought you liked that tune.

CEDRIC (*still* R. *of the piano; very earnestly*). Listen. I want you,

Sarah. You know that, don't you? And I want us to belong properly—by marriage.

SARAH. But you did promise——

CEDRIC. Only as an alternative to losing you altogether. . . . I confess that what you told me of Helen and Roger did make me feel we'd be justified in, at any rate, hesitating. But their attitude to each other this afternoon seems to have knocked the bottom out of that.

SARAH (*carelessly*). Aha?

CEDRIC (*leaning still further over the piano—very eagerly*). Sarah, let's risk it! Please! Forget all about that lovers' leap of yours; just shut your eyes, hold on to me, and take the jump!

(*She is thoughtful for a moment, seems about to speak, then changes her mind and shakes her head slowly but defiantly.*)

SARAH. Monday morning, Cedric.

CEDRIC (*straightening—disappointedly*). Oh—it's such a damn silly waste of time.

(SARAH *makes no reply. Her right hand drops to the keyboard and she commences to extemporize, slowly and meditatively, descending chords imitative of church bells.* CEDRIC *is about to add something further, when* ROGER, *wearing a dinner-suit, comes downstairs.*)

SARAH (*as he enters*). Hullo, Darby! Where's Joan?

ROGER. If you mean Helen, I tapped on her door as I passed, and she said she'd be down in a moment. (*Then with a quick change to a boisterous manner.*) But why are you two frowsting in here? Why aren't you in the garden watching the moon rise? (*To* CEDRIC.) Eh? (*He crosses down to* CEDRIC.)

CEDRIC (*crossing* R.). Oh—is there one?

ROGER. Is there one! Just you go and see if there isn't!

SARAH (*playing the piano*). I always have an inclination to take myself far too seriously when I look at the moon.

ROGER. That's funny. So do I. . . . Just now, as I sat looking out of my bedroom window, those lines of old Omar leapt to my mind: "How oft hereafter, rising, shall she look through this same garden after me in vain." A sad thought; and at the same time a happy one. For it made me think of all the years that are still left to us, with Helen and me growing older and older together.

SARAH. Interesting.

ROGER. Yes. (*To* CEDRIC.) I thought so too. Don't you find something almost hauntingly beautiful in the thought of two people —married people, of course—drifting into old age together, getting older and older?

CEDRIC. I do!

ROGER. So do I. . . . I think Helen will look lovely with silvery white hair, don't you, Sarah?

SARAH (*sotto voce*). It's a wonder it isn't that now.

ROGER. I beg your pardon?

SARAH (*pointedly*). It's a wonder it isn't that now.

ROGER (*ignoring this*). I pictured the two of us, walking slowly along the garden paths, hand in hand, each year a little slower.

(SARAH *plays and sings* "*My Old Dutch.*")

And I suddenly realized how wonderful life is. (*Then more brightly.*) However—just you take my advice, both of you, and look at that moon. Off with you! (*He crosses to* SARAH *at the piano.*)

CEDRIC (*eagerly, moving* C.). Sarah, please——

SARAH. You really want to, Cedric?

CEDRIC. I'd adore to.

SARAH (*rising*). Oh, very well. (*She crosses* ROGER *and goes* R. *to the library door. To* CEDRIC.) If we don't go of our own accord, he's quite capable of throwing us out. Come along. Not that way; we'll go through the library and out on to the terrace.

CEDRIC. Oh——

ROGER. That's right; you'll enjoy yourselves!

(CEDRIC *hurries* R., *opens the library door for her to pass through, then follows, closing the door behind him.*

The moment he finds himself alone, ROGER, *in the manner of an actor stepping out of an arduous rôle, relaxes. After a glance towards the door through which they have gone, he helps himself to a cigarette from the table* R.C., *lights it, then strolls in a leisurely manner across* L. *The wireless set engages his attention. He examines it curiously, then rather gingerly he twists one of the knobs. Instantly a blare of orchestral music leaps from it: a stirring Pomp and Circumstance sort of piece that crashes to a fortissimo wave of sound as* HELEN *appears at top of staircase and stands dramatically revealed. Her entrance is indeed so theatrical as to convey the impression that she has deliberately seized upon this particular moment to make it so. Her appearance, too, is well calculated to heighten the effect, for she has obviously taken the greatest pains with her toilette. Her dress one hesitates to describe. Sufficient to say that it is the very latest and most glittering "bon mot" whispered by the rustling silks of the Paris salons: a shimmering, iridescent affair of lace and sequins. As his back is turned to her he remains for a moment unaware. He turns towards staircase during music and sees* HELEN, *who moves down stage slowly, and with that grace of carriage which such a gown demands of its wearer.*)

HELEN (L. *of the stairs, with a gesture towards the wireless*). Won't you turn it off, Roger?

(*Dumbly he obeys, then turns to her again, seems as though trying to speak, but can only continue to stare. Then:*)

ROGER (*half under his breath*). Good Lord!

HELEN. What?
ROGER. You look—you look——
HELEN. Oh, this dress? You like it?
ROGER (*still staring at her*). Like it?
HELEN (*speaking rather rapidly*). I picked it up in Paris. Of course, it's much too elaborate for dinner; but I had a sudden silly whim to wear it. . . .
ROGER (*going up to her*). I'm glad you did. You look—marvellous!
HELEN (*with a rather shaky little laugh*). I warn you, Roger, that flattery goes straight to my head these days. . . . Come, now, be sensible and tell me——
ROGER (C.). No woman who looks as wonderful as you do has the right to ask a man to be sensible.
HELEN. Will you please stop talking like a Frederic Lonsdale duke and tell me where they are, at once?
ROGER (*recovering himself with an effort*). They?—— Oh, I sent them out to look at the moon.
HELEN (*approvingly*). That was very clever of you.
ROGER. Yes, I thought so too. And before that I managed to work off a rather telling bit about you and I growing senile together.
HELEN. Did it go down well?
ROGER. I think so.
HELEN. Good . . . I suppose they didn't happen to show the way the wind's blowing, so to speak?
ROGER (L.C.). Not in so many words, but as I entered this room, Sarah was seated at the piano giving an imitation of wedding bells.
HELEN. That sounds promising, don't you think?
ROGER. Well, she was certainly putting a good deal of feeling into it.
HELEN (*delightedly*). I really believe we have every cause to congratulate ourselves. . . . (*She crosses to* L. *of the settee*) . . . so far . . . Let me say at once, that I'm more than grateful to you, Roger.
ROGER (*moving down* C.). Oh, please.
HELEN (R.C.). All the more so when I think how you hated the idea. It's been splendid, the way you've disguised your real feelings and pretended, simply splendid.
ROGER. Oh—well—there hasn't been as much disguise about it as all that! It's true I hated the idea at first; and during tea, when we were inventing all that stuff, it wasn't too easy; but, somehow or other, since then I—well—I seem to have begun to enjoy it.
HELEN (*shaking her head disbelievingly*). Ah, I know you're saying that to please me.
ROGER. But I'm not! I mean it!

HELEN (*still disbelievingly*). Now, Roger. (*Then continuing quickly, to change the subject; moving a little away from him.*) I wonder, by the way, if either of them saw us by the fishpond.

ROGER. As we moved away I could almost swear I saw the curtains move at Norreys' window.

HELEN. Good. I'd hate to think it had been wasted. Standing for any length of time, with your head on someone else's shoulder, is a thoroughly overrated pastime. I still have a slight crick in the neck.

ROGER. I can't subscribe to that sentiment. It was when we were standing there, in fact, that I began to realize how much I was liking it.

HELEN. Oh! (*Sitting on the settee; brightly.*) Oh, well, tell me, have you brought down those photographs you promised to show me?

ROGER (*vaguely*). Photographs?

HELEN. Yes, the photographs.

ROGER (*remembering*). Oh—they're in my pocket. (*Sitting beside her, on her* L.) But you can look at them some other time.

HELEN. No, no! Now! at once! Why, I'm so anxious to see if Emily's as lovely as I feel sure she must be. Show them to me! Quickly!

ROGER. No, no!

HELEN. I must see them.

ROGER (*not very enthusiastically*). Oh, well! (*He fumbles in the pocket of his dinner-jacket and produces a leather wallet.*) I'm afraid they're mostly rather crude snapshots.

HELEN. Never mind. I always think snapshots are so much more true to life.

ROGER (*taking a photograph from the wallet*). Well—here's one of her seated on a camel.

(*She takes it from him very eagerly and studies it closely, holding it this way and that, as though to try the effect from various distances and angles. Then:*)

HELEN (*slowly*). Yes . . . I see . . . on a camel . . . yes . . . It isn't very clear, is it? (*As he stretches out his hand to take it from her.*) No, wait a minute. . . . Tell me, Roger, do all camels have that sort of sneering look, or does this particular one just happen to be feeling that way?

ROGER (*taking it from her*). Oh—they're all like that.

HELEN. I see.

ROGER (*producing another photograph*). Here's another one.

HELEN (*taking it and looking at it, then with a little gasp*). But, oh, my dear Roger, she's lovely!

ROGER. You—you really think so!

HELEN. Of course I do! But—why does it say Miss Gladys Cooper underneath?

Roger (*taking it from her quickly*). Oh—I'm so sorry. That's the wrong one; that's a postcard I bought last night, to get some change. (*Handing another from the wallet.*) Here—this is Emily.

Helen. Oh, yes . . . yes. . . . (*After a moment.*) Of course, she doesn't really favour Gladys Cooper at all, does she?

Roger. Did I ever say that she did?

Helen. No, dear, of course you didn't. I mean—it's not the same type of looks—if you understand me.

Roger (*stiffly*). Perfectly.

Helen (*hastily*). But very distinctive, Roger. Striking, you know. The sort of face that stamps on you—stamps itself on your memory, I mean. Not at all the pretty-pretty type that's here to-day and gone to-morrow. (*Still looking intently at the photograph.*) How old did you say she was?

Roger. I didn't say. But, since you ask me, I believe she's seen about thirty-five summers.

Helen. Summers! I see. Of course, if she's lived much in England, that may mean almost anything. (*She hands the photograph back to him.*) Well, go on, show me some more.

Roger. No!

Helen. Oh, but please!

Roger (*decisively, stuffing the wallet back into his pocket*). No, Helen. (*He rises and moves* c.)

Helen. Stubborn! You'll, at any rate, allow me to say that I hope she'll make you very happy. (*She rises and goes to him and puts his tie straight.*)

Roger. Thank you very much.

Helen. Would it be bad taste, do you think, for me to give you both a wedding present?

Roger. The worst possible, I should imagine.

Helen. Even if it were something quite simple? Nose-bags for the camels, for instance?

(*He stands quite still, regarding her, his consciousness again stirred and held by her appearance.*)

(*Growing a little self-conscious under his stare.*) They—they do wear nose-bags, I suppose?

Roger. Yes—no—— Oh, I don't know! . . . Helen——

Helen. Yes?

Roger (l.c.). Why do you always say the sort of things you know will irritate me?

Helen (c.). My dear, I don't mean to.

Roger. No, that's just it, I don't believe we either of us really meant to—those other times—and yet it happened.

Helen. So many times, Roger.

Roger. Oh, what a pity it all is! . . . Us, I mean.

Helen (*faintly*). Oh! . . . I—I think I ought to ring for the sherry. I'm sure they must have forgotten it. (*She crosses to the bell and rings.*)

Roger (*sitting on the book in the armchair* L.C.). Oh, damn! (*He throws the book on to the settee. After a pause; still looking at her.*) What a mess we've made of things, Helen. What an unholy mess.

Helen (*in a small voice*). Yes—I suppose we did.

Roger. To throw away our chance of happiness as we did. . . . Why *did* we do it?

Helen (*at the back of the settee*). But, Roger, you explained it all beautifully this afternoon : " An infinite capacity for loving one another."

Roger (*interrupting her almost savagely*). Oh, for Heaven's sake, don't start quoting what I said this afternoon ! (*After a short pause, getting up and moving round* L. *of the chair.*) I'm not at all sure the explanation we invented over the teacups wasn't the right one. . . . Intolerance—temperament, lack of understanding, and so on.

Helen. And so on.

Roger. Our chance came when we weren't ready for it. . . . If only it were being offered to us now ! How differently everything would turn out.

Helen. I wonder. (*She comes* C.)

Roger (*sitting on the* R. *arm of the chair*). I know. Because *we're* different. I know I've changed in all sorts of ways, and so have you.

Helen (*quickly*). Tell me how I've changed, please.

Roger. Oh, I don't know. . . . You're sort of . . . softer, I think.

Helen. Softer ? (*She sits on the* L. *arm of the settee.*)

Roger. I mean it in the nicest possible way, my dear. I remember you as a—(*with a descriptive gesture*) a perfect mass of prickles ; but to-night—why—there doesn't seem to be a solitary prickle left . . . sitting there, you're just like . . .

Helen. Yes ?

Roger. Like the woman I used to wish you would be, but grew tired of hoping you ever could be.

Helen. I see. (*After a pause.*) You'll not deny that you had a prickle or two yourself, Roger ?

Roger (*rising*). Oh, I had, I had ! (*He moves up* L.C.)

Helen. You neglected me shamefully for your Egyptology.

Roger (*turning up* L.C.). Not really, Helen. (*Moving down.*) It was only that you didn't understand.

Helen. Whether I did or not, that was the cause of *all* our worst quarrels.

Roger. Oh, come ; not quite all. I seem to remember several pretty spectacular outbursts that arose from some silliness, if you'll forgive me, on your part.

HELEN. Ho!

ROGER. As an instance: the ridiculous panic you used to be thrown into by the merest hint of a thunderstorm. (*He moves* L. *to the piano.*)

HELEN. Oh—well—perhaps that was a little tiresome of me. But I did hate them so.

ROGER. Don't you now?

HELEN. Now? (*Hesitating for a fraction of a second, then with a reckless laugh.*) Why, no—I adore them! (*She rises and moves up* C.)

ROGER (*staring at her*). You mean—they don't frighten you any more?

HELEN. Certainly not! (*Still more recklessly, turning up* C.) Why, whenever there's a really good one I go out on the roof to watch it!

ROGER (*behind the armchair*). On the roof!

HELEN (*moving down to behind the settee*). The thrill you get when you see the lightning playing round your head! I wouldn't miss it for worlds! The forked kind's the best, of course.

ROGER. And also the most dangerous.

HELEN. Rubbish, Roger! You always used to din it into me that thunderstorms weren't a bit dangerous.

ROGER. Nor they are, for those who realize the happy medium between standing on the roof and cowering in the boot-cupboard. (*After a pause.*) Still, it only goes to show. (*He sits on the* R. *arm of the chair.*)

HELEN. Show what?

ROGER. How you've changed, Helen. This afternoon I thought you were just the same, but since then I've realized.

ROGER }
HELEN } (*together*). Ah!

(*There is a pause.*)

ROGER (*shaking his head; sighing*). Life is very queer.

HELEN. May I ask what inspires that platitude?

ROGER. Merely the thought that I should find the woman who is about to divorce me so much more charming than the woman who married me.

HELEN. That's very nice of you, Roger. (*Moving round above the table to* C.) And if it convinces me of anything at all, it is that . . . (*She moves down* C.)

ROGER. Well?

HELEN. That though the dress I'm wearing was expensive, it was not too expensive.

ROGER (*rising*). What do you mean by that? (*He goes close to her.*)

HELEN (*with a little smile*). Only that I'm not sure whether you're being nice to me or to my clothes.

ROGER (*earnestly*). Nonsense! I assure you that I should be just as nice to you without them. (*He kisses her neck.*)

HELEN. Roger!

(*The next instant, with a clumsy movement, he grabs her shoulders and kisses her awkwardly.*)

(*Struggling to free herself.*) Oh—please! (*She breaks away.*)

(ROGER *looks abashed.*)

Really, for a man who's about to tell the world that nothing could ever induce him to live in the same house with me, your conduct is extraordinary!

ROGER (*lamely*). I'm sorry . . . I—I thought I heard the others coming, and that it would be a good thing if they caught us kissing.

HELEN (*looking at him very directly*). Did you?

ROGER. No. . . . I didn't. I'm very sorry. Please say you forgive me.

HELEN (*after a moment*). For kissing me, yes; for making excuses for doing so, no.

(*She flashes a smile at him, and he smiles back, relieved. The double doors* L. *open, and* POYNTER *comes in with a tray upon which are sherry and glasses. He puts them on the table* R.C.)

Ah, the sherry. (*She goes up* C.)

(POYNTER, *having placed the tray on the table, returns to the dining-room, closing the doors behind him.*)

(*Going to* L. *of the table.*) You'll have one?

ROGER (*down* L.). Please. (*Referring to* POYNTER.) Silent fellow! (*He goes* R. *and up to the table, round* R. *end of the settee.*)

HELEN (*as she pours out the sherry*). I've been thinking, if our little conspiracy proves successful, there'll be no need for you to stay here until they're actually married. You can say you have things to see to in Town, and I can invent some reason for not accompanying you.

ROGER (R. *of her*). But there's really no hurry. I haven't got to be in London. (*Accepting his glass from her.*) Thank you.

HELEN. But of course you've *got* to be! I can't write you a letter asking you to return to me if you're living in this house, can I?

ROGER. Oh . . . of course . . . I was forgetting. (*Bracing himself.*) Still, let's leave all that until Monday morning, shall we?

HELEN. If you say so, Roger.

ROGER (*in front of the table, gaily*). And what about you and I drinking a private little toast before the others return, eh?

HELEN (*enthusiastically*). Of course! (*Raising her glass.*) To Emily!

Sc. 1.]   LOVERS' LEAP.   49

ROGER (*quickly*). No, no!
HELEN. What?
ROGER. Er—Emily's a teetotaller.
HELEN. Oh, shall I ring for Poynter to bring the Ovaltine?
ROGER. We'll think of another toast.
HELEN. All right. Let's be unoriginal and just say " Happy days."
ROGER (*raising his glass*). Happy days!
(*They clink glasses and drink. There is a moment of silence. Then :*)
(*Beginning with sudden intense earnestness.*) Helen—— (*Then breaking off abruptly.*)
HELEN. Yes?

(*There is the sound of voices off.*)

ROGER. I—I——
HELEN. Ssh! I hear them!
ROGER (*under his breath*). Blast! (*He crosses down* L.)

(*The library door opens, and* SARAH, *followed by* CEDRIC, *comes in.* CEDRIC *with powder on his shoulder.*)

HELEN (*brightly*). Ah, here you are, then!
SARAH. Yes, dear. We're ravenously hungry. Can we have dinner soon? (*She crosses down* R.)
HELEN (*moving to* C.). Two minutes, darling. There's sherry there——
SARAH. Lovely! (*To* CEDRIC.) Get me one, dear, will you?

(CEDRIC *goes to the table.*)

ROGER (*to* CEDRIC). Well, Norreys, what about that moon, eh?
CEDRIC (*pouring out drinks*). All that you led us to believe—and more.
SARAH. Oh, it's simply stifling out there!
CEDRIC. I didn't notice the heat. (*He crosses to her, a glass in either hand.*)
SARAH (*down* R.). And those beastly midges droning about all over the place, and taking the most obscene liberties with one. (*She takes her glass from him and sits on the stool at the desk.*)
CEDRIC. I didn't notice the midges, either.
HELEN. Of course you didn't.
ROGER (*crossing to behind the settee—to* CEDRIC). Excuse me. (*With one hand he brushes from* CEDRIC'S *shoulder a large patch of powder.*)
CEDRIC. Er—thank you. Really, I wonder what it can be.
HELEN (*knowingly, above the table* R.C.). Ah, I wonder.
SARAH (*sipping her sherry*). For God's sake stop being arch, Helen. It's powder off my face, of course.

(ROGER *gives* CEDRIC *a jovial dig in the ribs, while* HELEN *shakes a roguish finger.*)

D

ROGER. Aha!—aha!—aha!
SARAH. When you've quite finished knocking Cedric about, he was only showing me how he saw you two standing by the fishpond earlier in the evening.
HELEN (*eagerly*). Ah, you *did* see us, then?
(*Unobserved, she and* ROGER *exchange a swift glance.*)
CEDRIC (*hastily*). Please don't think I was meaning to——
ROGER (*cutting him short—boisterously*). Oh, we don't mind, do we, Helen?
(HELEN *shakes her head and smiles.*)
SARAH. Obviously not, or you'd have chosen a less public place than in full view of the windows. Cedric was most impressed.
ROGER (*moving to down* L.). Splendid!
SARAH. It is not splendid. The poor darling's been so wrought-up and emotional ever since, there's no doing anything with him. (*She drinks.*)
CEDRIC (*above* R. *end of the settee*). Oh, I say, I hope you don't believe that.
HELEN (*animatedly*). But why not? (*Moving down* R.) I adore people who aren't ashamed to be emotional. Look at me! I'm ecstatically happy to-night, and do I care who knows it? (*Blowing* ROGER *a kiss.*) There, darling! (*She sits* R. *on the settee.*)
ROGER (*wafting a kiss in return*). Dearest!
(SARAH *gives a shrill little laugh, instantly checked as she catches* HELEN'S *eye.*)
SARAH. Sorry, darling. (*She drains her glass.*)
HELEN. But why, dear, why? (*With a gesture.*) Laugh as much as you like. Roger and I don't mind a bit. Do we, dearest?
ROGER (*moving* R.). On the contrary, I love to hear your sister laugh; she can't do that and talk at the same time. (*He sits* L. *on the settee, but on the book. With an angry movement he throws the book on to the armchair* L.C.)
HELEN (*leaning affectionately against* ROGER; *sighing happily*). Oh dear, oh dear, oh dear!
SARAH. What's wrong now?
HELEN. Wrong? (*With a little laugh.*) I was just thinking how beautifully right everything was——
SARAH. Oh!
HELEN (*breaking off—to* ROGER). Not hurting your arm, am I?
ROGER. Not a bit.
HELEN. Not a teeny weeny little bit?
ROGER. Not a teeny weeny little bit.
HELEN (*hunching her shoulders and snuggling still closer to him*). How true it is that, when all's said and done, happiness is the only thing that really matters.

(ROGER *takes her hand and presses it silently.*)

It is, you take my word.

SARAH. Your word? I'm wondering if I oughtn't to take your temperature.

HELEN (*continuing*). And yet, the millions and millions of people who go on through life, just muddling their chances, or letting them slip by. So very, very sad. (*Looking up at* ROGER.) M'm?

ROGER. Oh—tragic, very.

HELEN. They simply don't know what they want.

CEDRIC (*abruptly*). There's no doubt in my—— (*He breaks off.*)

SARAH. Yes, dear? Speak up.

CEDRIC. Nothing.

SARAH. Oh, please.

CEDRIC (*rather hesitatingly*). Well—I was about to say—there's no doubt in my mind as to what I want.

HELEN (*sitting up*). Then you see that you get it, my dear Cedric, see that you get it.

(*The doors* L. *are flung open, and* POYNTER *enters.*)

POYNTER. Dinner is served, madam.

HELEN (*rising*). Oh, thank you, Poynter.

(ROGER *and* SARAH *rise.*)

(POYNTER *returns to the dining-room.*)

HELEN (*going to* CEDRIC). Dinner, Cedric. I expect you're ravenous.

CEDRIC. Knowing that dinner will be as perfect as everything is in your house, I am.

HELEN (*taking his arm*). Come along, then.

(*They go towards the dining-room.*)

(*With a swift change to a bright conversational tone.*) And now, I want you to tell me *all* about your house in Scotland. I expect it's simply too grim and exciting, with mountains and heather and stags and——

(*They have gone off* L., *and her voice is now only heard as a faint rippling murmur.*)

ROGER, *standing up* L., *crooks his arm invitingly towards* SARAH. *The latter hesitates a second; then, with a toss of her head, she sweeps past him and into the dining-room. There is the sound of* HELEN'S *laughter rising higher and higher, and, after a moment, a long, low rumble of distant thunder, muttering, rolling, seeming about to rise to a crashing climax, then suddenly dying away.* ROGER, *with an amused cock of the eyebrows, follows the others into the dining-room.*)

CURTAIN.

Scene 2

The Curtain *remains down for no more than a minute or two to represent the passage of one hour. While it is still down, the wireless is heard broadcasting dance music.*

The Curtain *rises.* Cedric *and* Sarah *are upstage dancing solemnly to the music.* Roger *is sitting* R. *on the settee, smoking a cigar, a coffee-cup in his right hand, the saucer on the arm of the settee. He is staring dreamily and unseeingly in front of him, apparently in a state of after-dinner contentment.* Helen *is sitting on the* R. *arm of the settee, above* Roger's *saucer, sipping her coffee.*

Wireless. You have just been listening to a fox-trot entitled "Let's Fall in Love." We are now going to play you another fox-trot, "Going to Get Another Baby."

Sarah. Oh, no, you're not. (*She crosses to the wireless and switches it off.*) It's too hot to dance, anyway.

Helen. I'm afraid the floor isn't very good.

Cedric (L.C.). Oh, but it's quite good, really.

Sarah (*to him*). What do you know about the floor? You've been dancing on my feet all the time.

Cedric. Sorry, Sarah. It's that new step I can't quite get the hang of.

Sarah. My dear, a child of two could do it. Let me show you.

(*They go up* C. *on to the rostrum, and all one hears from them for the next few minutes are:* "No, no, one step to the right, and then turn." "Don't look at your feet." "Now the left. No, the left." "Oh, why will you look at your feet?" "And turn on your right heel." *And so on. While they are absorbed in this,* Helen *nudges* Roger, *and accidentally knocks the ash from his cigar.*)

Roger. Now, dear, just look what you've done!

Helen (*in a very breathy whisper, so as not to be overheard*). My dear, I haven't had a chance to tell you before, but I think you were perfectly splendid at dinner! Simply splendid, Roger! I'm sure even Sarah was impressed. And as for Cedric, he just drank it in.

Roger (*with a little reminiscent smile*). He did rather mop it up, didn't he? (*Adding.*) You were pretty good yourself, Helen, if it comes to that.

Helen (*after another glance at the other two*). If you ask me, we've as good as won. Just look at them now. One could almost imagine them husband and wife already. (*She jolts* Roger's *coffee-cup.*)

Roger. I say, steady, my dear, look out! (*He steals a covert glance at the two over his shoulder.*)

Sarah (*at that moment, giving* Cedric *a little shake*). My dear idiot, if you'd only try to do *exactly* as I tell you.

(HELEN *gets up and looks at* SARAH *and* CEDRIC.)

ROGER. H'm! One certainly could.

HELEN (*at the back of the settee*). I don't mind telling you that Sarah has caused me quite a lot of anxiety just lately. And when she arrived here this afternoon and calmly announced she was thinking of *living* with him. . . .

ROGER. Oh, quite.

HELEN (*sitting on the back of the settee*). Well, I mean, as an elder sister, one has one's responsibilities. (*Leaning closer to him.*) I can't tell you what a relief it would be to see her married and settled. And if she does, it's you she'll have to thank.

ROGER (*modestly*). Oh, I say.

HELEN. No, no. Alone, I couldn't have done a thing. Not a thing.

ROGER. M'm! I wonder if Cedric will thank me.

HELEN. Why not? Aren't you helping him to get what he wants more than anything in the world? Aren't we helping them both through our—our innocent little machinations?

(SARAH *and* CEDRIC *exit* L. *on the rostrum.*)

ROGER. Little what?

HELEN (*close to his ear*). Machinations.

ROGER (*rubbing his ear violently*). Darling, I do wish you wouldn't hiss words like that right into my ear.

HELEN. I *am* so sorry. But you see what I mean, don't you? (*She jolts him a little with her shoulder.*)

ROGER (*balancing his cup again*). I see one thing quite clearly, and that is, you're going to have this coffee all over me if you aren't careful.

HELEN. Well, why not drink it and put the cup down?

ROGER. Because I like to sip my coffee and not to swill it—do you mind?

HELEN. Not a bit.

(*He gives a little laugh.*)

What's the matter?

ROGER. I just remembered—a fellow I met on the boat. He told me his wife was the clumsiest woman in the world. (*With another little laugh.*) I told him I knew a clumsier.

HELEN. What?

ROGER. Well, you always were, you know.

HELEN (*standing*). I? Well, I must say I like that! Why, I never——

ROGER. Oh, now, come, come, Helen, what about that set of Venetian glass finger-bowls that you smashed steadily, one after another?

HELEN. Oh, those! I always hated them, anyway. (*She crosses down* L.)

Roger. As it happens, I liked them. They were a wedding present from Sir Cyprian Musk, one of the greatest authorities on the Ethiopian dynasty.

Helen. And also the greatest bore, dear. (*Moving* c.) And I do think, darling, it was rather unkind of you to talk of me to your friend as though I were some great galumphing elephant.

Roger. Elephants, my dear, are not a bit clumsy. Don't you know that an elephant can pick up a pin with its trunk?

(Sarah *and* Cedric *re-enter up* L.)

A man I knew in Alexandria once told me——

Helen (*at* L. *end of the settee*). Oh, all right, all right! Now, Roger, don't let's argue about elephants. It's much too hot.

Roger. I wasn't arguing. I was only——

Helen. Well, don't let's even *talk* about them. (*Sitting on the settee beside him.*) Give me a kiss quickly. . . . They're looking straight at us.

Roger. What? Oh—— (*He kisses her somewhat perfunctorily.*)

Helen. Angel, that was sweet of you. All the same, I think it was rather beastly of you to describe me as an elephant.

(Sarah *and* Cedric *come down stage.*)

Roger. I did not describe you as an elephant.

Helen. But you said——

Roger. My dear Helen, the word "elephant" never crossed my lips.

Helen (*in a hurried whisper*). Sst! They're coming over here. Let's be talking. (*In a much louder tone.*) Let me take your cup—darling.

Roger. What? (*Rising.*) I can put it down myself, thank you . . . er—angel. (*He puts his cup on the table* R.C.)

(Sarah *and* Cedric *have come down* L. Sarah *sits in the armchair.*)

Sarah. Believe me or believe me not, my little Cedric does not know his left foot from his right.

Cedric (*down* L.). I do, Sarah, but I get nervous.

Sarah. All right, darling, all right!

Helen (*to* Roger). Another liqueur, darling?

Roger. No, thank you—precious. (*He puts his cigar out in an ashtray on the table.*)

Sarah (*rising*). I will. (*She goes to the table* R.C.) Brandy, Cedric?

Cedric. Thank you, no.

Sarah (*pouring out a drink*). Helen?

Helen (*shaking her head*). I never have more than one.

(Roger *goes up* R. *to the bookshelves.*)

Sarah. What you miss! I love the good things of life. (*She drinks, smiling towards* CEDRIC.) All right, dear, you needn't look so self-conscious.

CEDRIC. I was just wishing that I might always be to you what brandy is to Helen.

SARAH (*looking at* HELEN). What *can* he mean by that?

CEDRIC. I mean, one of the things you'd never have more than one of.

SARAH (*with a little laugh*). He says the quaintest things. (*To him.*) We'll see, my sweet, we'll see.

ROGER (*studying the titles of the books*). What a truly appalling collection of books, Helen. Do you never, by any chance, read about anything but love?

SARAH. One must keep in touch, Roger. (*She puts her glass down on the table.*) You ought to be glad she's been content merely to read about it, these past seven years. (*She moves down and sits in the armchair again with a periodical taken from the table.*)

HELEN (*frowning at* SARAH). The kind you like are all in the library, dearest. (*Rising.*) Really, the heat to-night is unbearable.

CEDRIC. Still, the thunder seems to have passed off, doesn't it?

HELEN (*down* C., *quickly*). Thunder? I never heard any thunder.

SARAH. I did.

CEDRIC. Just as we were sitting down to dinner.

HELEN. Oh! (*Then with a swift glance towards* ROGER—*sitting on the settee.*) Really? Just fancy. (*She takes up a newspaper.*)

CEDRIC (*reassuringly*). Still, I'm sure you've no occasion to feel nervous.

ROGER (*coming down stage*). What d'you mean—nervous? Hey? Are you suggesting that my wife is one of those flibbertygibberty women who are thrown into a funk by a mere thunderstorm?

CEDRIC (*dimly conscious that he has said the wrong thing*). Well —er—some are, you know.

ROGER (*scornfully*). I've no patience with the weak-minded fools! Recently I heard of a woman who used to be thrown into such a state of panic by a thunderstorm, she'd actually crawl away and hide in the boot-cupboard! I ask you!

CEDRIC (*timidly*). Well, I myself have an aunt who——

ROGER (*impatiently*). Never mind about your aunt; listen to me. Now she enjoys them, actually goes out on the roof to watch 'em! On the roof, Norreys.

CEDRIC. Good gracious!

SARAH. Good God! What do you think of that, Helen?

HELEN (*pretending to be absorbed in her paper*). I—er—yes, of course.

CEDRIC (*down* L.). Still, one does hear of cases. You must listen to this.

ROGER. Oh, must I?

CEDRIC. In the town where my aunt lives, a woman sitting quietly in her own home, reading her evening newspaper, was struck dead by lightning.

(HELEN *starts violently and hastily discards the newspaper.*)

ROGER. Of course such things do happen, but talking of this woman friend of mine, she's going to have the treat of her life to-night. (*He laughs.*)

HELEN (*nervously, but striving not to appear so*). Oh—er—why, dear?

ROGER (*going up to the window and drawing back the curtains*). Because, if I'm any judge of weather, there's a devil of a storm piling up at this moment. Can't you feel it in the air?

CEDRIC (*glancing towards* HELEN—*uneasily*). It certainly is unusually warm.

ROGER (*moving* L.). I give it no more than half an hour before it bursts on us. You mark my words.

(CEDRIC *comes to* C. HELEN, *who has been sitting absolutely rigid, listening, rises, goes to the table to get a drink.*)

CEDRIC. If you're right, then you—your friend must be looking forward to a thoroughly enjoyable evening.

ROGER (*to him*). I can picture her now, bless her brave heart, thinking of reaching for her mackintosh and sou'wester in readiness.

(HELEN *grasps the decanter and pours some brandy into her glass.*)

SARAH (*in the armchair* L.C., *glancing up from her periodical*). Hullo! I thought you never had more than one.

ROGER. Anything the matter, dear? (*He crosses* CEDRIC *to* L. *of the table.*)

HELEN (*with ghastly brightness*). No—of course not. (*With a little laugh.*) Nothing. (*She gives another little laugh.*)

ROGER. Good!

(HELEN *goes to* R. *of the settee with her half-empty glass.* CEDRIC *moves* L.)

Just having another one!

(ROGER *takes his cigarette-case from his pocket, and she quickly gulps the remainder.* SARAH *gives a sudden gurgle of laughter.*)

SARAH. Tell me, Roger, anything you may happen to know about Lady Emily Willock.

ROGER (C., *starting and dropping his cigarette-case*). What? (*He stoops to pick up his case.*)

HELEN (*who has also started; turning*). Why—why should he know anything about her?

SARAH. Well, she's described here as an Egyptologist, like himself. (*To* ROGER.) Do you know her?

ROGER. I've . . . heard of her.
SARAH. Heard of her! My God! You ought to see her face. (*She rises.*)

(*A look passes between* HELEN *and* ROGER.)

ROGER. Lady Emily Willock, it may interest you to know, has done research work of incalculable value in Egypt.

SARAH (*crossing* R. *to* HELEN). Aha ? So now we know why the sands of the desert grow cold. Look at it! Did you ever see anything so utterly Whipsnade ?

(ROGER *goes up* C.)

HELEN (*taking the periodical and studying it*). Oh—I don't agree with you, Sarah.

SARAH. You don't mean to tell me you find that face pleasing ?

HELEN (*viewing the page at arm's length*). I can't tell you how much it pleases me, Sarah. (*Handing it back to her.*) Show it to Roger, dear, and see if he doesn't agree with me.

SARAH. You're mad. (*Crossing up to* ROGER *and thrusting the periodical into his hands.*) Here—if you can bear it.

CEDRIC (*moving up* L., *peering over* ROGER'S *shoulder, then laughing*). By Jove ! I say ! Looks like a street accident, don't you think ?

ROGER (*frowning at the photograph*). No, sir, I do not. Since you ask my opinion, I think she's a devilish handsome-looking woman.

HELEN. There ! You see !

SARAH. You're insane, both of you.

HELEN (*moving to* C.). For instance, although Lady Emily what's-her-name's face pleases me enormously, I do *not* think she favours Gladys Cooper.

(SARAH *shouts with laughter.*)

ROGER (*pitching the periodical on to the table*). No one but a damned fool would ever dream of comparing the two !

HELEN (*crossing to* R. *of the settee*). No, dear, that's what I say.

ROGER (*moving down to* L. *of her*). Then, why do it ? Why ? Why ? Why ?

HELEN. Darling, darling, there's no need to get excited.

ROGER. I am not in the least excited, (*gulping*) angel. (*He turns* L.)

HELEN. I was merely explaining that different types——

(*She breaks off as a peal of thunder is heard, not very loud, though considerably louder than that which occurred at the end of Scene* 1.)

ROGER. Ha ! . . . You hear that ? (*Triumphantly.*) What did I tell you ? (*He goes up* C.)

HELEN (*in front of the settee, starting, then controlling herself*). Was that thunder ?

ROGER. What did you think it was?

(HELEN *moves up to above the table.*)

CEDRIC (*reassuringly, addressing himself indirectly to* HELEN). I expect it's a long way off, really, and probably it won't come any nearer.

ROGER (*at the window*). Nonsense! It's just rushing closer and closer upon us every minute. Just you wait!

CEDRIC. But it may——

SARAH (*taking* CEDRIC'S *arm, coming* R. *and sitting on the settee*). Oh, don't argue with him about it. It's his storm. (*To* HELEN.) And, darling, why don't you sit down? You look so——

(*There is a flash of lightning.*)

ROGER (*as lightning flickers across the hall window*). Ha!—See that?

HELEN (*up stage* R.C., *stifling a scream*). What?—Where?

ROGER. Lightning. Fork lightning. Ha!

(*There is a second flash.*)

HELEN (*her voice unnaturally high and strained*). Well, I do wish you wouldn't keep saying "Ha!" like that.

ROGER. Ssh!—Wait!—Wait!

(*A peal of thunder, louder than before.*)

There! That's much nearer.

HELEN (*faintly*). Much.

CEDRIC (*at* L. *end of the settee*). But not so near as it sounds, I'm sure.

(*Thunder rumbles.*)

ROGER (*coming down stage*). It's possible, of course, to calculate pretty accurately the distance of the storm-centre, by timing the interval between the lightning and the thunder.

HELEN (*breathlessly, to conceal her nervousness*). No, really? Isn't that marvellous? Science, these days! (*Moving down* R. *of the settee.*) Sarah, did you know that you could do that?

SARAH. Yes, I did. And I do wish you'd sit down.

HELEN (*with the sharpness of taut nerves*). Do, please, stop telling me to sit down, dear. I—I'm perfectly happy as I am. (*She moves in front of the settee to* C.)

SARAH (*looking at her*). Are you?

ROGER. Wait! Everybody wait for the next flash, and then count.

SARAH. I never can after dinner. Sorry. Just twiddle one of those knobs, will you, Cedric, and see what the wireless is doing!

(CEDRIC *goes to the wireless down* L. HELEN *sits in the armchair* L.C. ROGER *has moved up stage, and is gazing with great concentration towards the window.* CEDRIC *turns a knob on the wireless set and is immediately rewarded with a deafening blare of sound; a brass band playing* " *The Ride of the Valkyries.*" SARAH *presses her hands over her ears.*)

CEDRIC (*shouting*). Don't you like it?

(HELEN *shakes her head violently.*)

HELEN (*shouting, as he is about to turn it off*). No! No! Leave it on! Leave it on!

(*Lightning. A flicker across the window.*)

ROGER (*at window, yelling*). There! One—two—three—four——

(*Thunder. A loud peal.*)

HELEN (*jumping up*). Aaah!

ROGER (*whipping round to face her*). What's the matter with you?

(*She gesticulates wildly towards the wireless set.* CEDRIC *hesitates bewilderedly, then turns it off.*)

CEDRIC. But I thought you wanted it on.
HELEN. Disconnect it, please.

(CEDRIC *obeys at once.*)

(*With an effort, contriving a breathless little laugh.*) Thank you, Cedric. I don't think we must have it on just now. I suddenly remembered that it's supposed to be dangerous when there's lightning about.

ROGER (C.). Nonsense!

HELEN (*moving* R. *a little*). No, really, Roger. . . . In fact, I'm not sure there isn't something about it in the insurance policy. (*Then adding lamely, conscious that* ROGER *is staring at her very fixedly.*) Insurance people are so funny, aren't they?

ROGER (*still staring at her, almost as though a suspicion is forming in his mind*). Damned funny. . . . H'm! (*Looking away from her.*) I counted up to four. But unless I'm very much mistaken, that means that the full force of the storm is concentrated over this house. (*He points to the ceiling.*)

HELEN (*coming* C., *scarcely audible*). Oh!

SARAH. Thank you so much for telling us, Roger.

CEDRIC. That means that from now onwards it'll be moving farther and farther away from us.

HELEN (*wanly*). Yes—yes, of course.

(*Lightning. Thunder.*)

ROGER. Well, I don't know. I believe that sometimes a storm will stay practically stationary overhead for hours.

(*Thunder.*)

HELEN (*under her breath*). Oh, God!

(*There is a loud reverberating crash of thunder.* HELEN, *terrified, claps her hand over her mouth, then, conscious that* ROGER *is watching her, by a great effort, she pulls herself together and pretends to be stifling a yawn. Rain starts.*)

ROGER (*as the thunder dies away*). Sleepy, darling?
HELEN. No—oh, no, dear—not a bit sleepy. (*She crosses to* R. *of the settee.*)
ROGER. That's good. Quite happy? (*He moves* R. *a little.*)
HELEN (*forcing a smile*). Quite . . . darling.
ROGER (*his glance still lingering on her*). Splendid!
CEDRIC. Is that rain I can hear? By Jove! (*He crosses up* L.C.)

(*The rain is heard lashing against the window. They all listen.*)

SARAH. What a filthy night!
CEDRIC (*at the window*). Filthy!

(ROGER *smiles to himself, then commences to laugh. Lightning.*)

HELEN (*apprehensively*). What's the matter, Roger?
ROGER (*moving up to* CEDRIC *and speaking through his laughter*). I was thinking of—of all those women who at this moment are hiding in wardrobes. (*He laughs still louder.*) Or cowering in—in boot-cupboards!

(*Thunder. He laughs uproariously.* HELEN, *after a moment, joins in very half-heartedly.*)

(*Still laughing.*) Boot-cupboards, Norreys.
CEDRIC. Er—yes—very amusing.
HELEN. Let's do something, shall we? How about one of those paper games?
ROGER. Not for me, thank you.

(*Lightning.*)

HELEN. Oh, yes! You write down an author's name and the title of the book, and it's all quite mad and terribly amusing—isn't it, Sarah? I'll get some paper.

(*Thunder.*)

CEDRIC. I say, wouldn't you like to go to your room?
HELEN (*sharply, clinging desperately to her ebbing self-control*). Why should I? (*She is down* R.)

Roger (*up* c.). Do you know, Helen, I believe he thinks you're nervous. (*Laughing.*) Oh, that's funny, that's damned funny!

Sarah. Oh, shut up, Roger!

Roger (c., *still laughing*). Great heavens! Am I the only person in this house with a sense of humour? Perhaps you'll laugh when I tell you that Helen is the woman I was speaking of just now—the woman who enjoys thunderstorms, revels in them!

Cedric (*moving down slightly*). But——

Roger (c.). Frightened! What an idea! Why, if it weren't for her duties as a hostess she'd be out on the roof, having the time of her life! Wouldn't you, Helen? (*He crosses to* Helen, r.)

Helen (*weakly*). Yes——

Roger. Yes, I know, darling, and it's a shame. But you shall see the pretty lightning. (*As she tries to speak.*) Just one moment while I switch off the light.

(*Before anyone has time to say anything, he has hurried to the switch by the library door. Click! The room is in darkness. Lightning.*)

Sarah. Roger, you're not to! Cedric——

Roger (*springing up the two steps into the rostrum*). Now we shan't be long.

(*Lightning. Thunder.* Helen, *moving up stage, screams hysterically as the darkness is rent by a terrific flash. The lights in the room go up.* Helen, *panting, her breast heaving, one hand still clutching the switch by the library door, is standing with her back to the wall.* Roger *is facing her.* Cedric, *quite aghast, is standing down* l. *by the armchair.* Sarah *up* r. *by bookcase.*)

(*By the window, with a little mocking smile.*) Why, Helen, is anything the matter?

Helen (*running down* r. *to the settee, half-sobbing with rage and fear*). Matter? You beast! Oh, you beast!

Roger (*with exaggerated amazement*). Here, I say, I say! What's——

(*Thunder. His voice is drowned by an appalling crash.* Helen *flings herself face downwards on the settee, her head half-buried among the cushions, her toes drumming hysterically.* Sarah *hurries to the back of the settee and bends over her solicitously.*)

Sarah (*as the thunder dies away*). There, there, darling, it's quite all right, it isn't going to hurt you. (*To* Roger.) You cad!

Roger (*who has come down stage*). What's all the fuss about? (*Appealing to* Cedric.) Norreys, I ask you, have I done anything to justify my being called a cad?

(Helen *buries her head in the cushions again and moans, lying prone on settee.*)

Cedric (l.c.). Since you ask me—yes.

ROGER. But I only——
CEDRIC (*above armchair* L.C.). You know that your wife is terrified of storms, and yet you deliberately——
ROGER. I know nothing of the sort. It's little more than an hour ago that in this very room she was assuring me she——
HELEN (*springing to her knees on the settee*). Hold your tongue, will you?
ROGER (*turning to her*). But did you or did you not tell me——
HELEN. Never mind what I told you, you loathsome bully!

(*Lightning.*)

ROGER. You mean, you were lying to me? Aha! I see. It was very, very naughty of you, Helen.

(*Thunder.*)

HELEN. Oh, shut up, before I——

(*A flash of lightning.* HELEN *dives among the cushions.*)

Oh, my God! Don't let it touch me! Don't let it!
ROGER (*to* CEDRIC). She means the lightning. (*To* HELEN.) Well, well, this is quite like old times, I must say. But hadn't you better remember we've guests in the house and try to pull yourself together?

(*Lightning.*)

HELEN (*not raising her head; very muffled*). I don't care if the Prince of Wales is in the house! Oh, why doesn't it go away? Oh! oh! oh! (*She presses cushions over her ears, drums again with her toes, and wails.*)

(*Thunder.*)

SARAH. Quiet, dear, quiet.
ROGER. A pretty exhibition, I must say. (*With a contemptuous wave of the hand towards the prostrate* HELEN.) We might be back in the Stone Age.
SARAH (*viciously*). If we were, I'd give you one over the head with a club.
ROGER (*coming to* L. *end of settee and raising his eyebrows slightly*). Really! (*Then ignoring her, grasping* HELEN'S *shoulder a little and shaking her.*) Helen, will you kindly stop this ridiculous nonsense. You hear me, Helen?

(HELEN'S *only response is to wriggle more convulsively and to moan unintelligibly into the cushions.*)

(*With a gesture—to* CEDRIC.) You see? No reasoning with her at all.
SARAH (*bending over her*). Darling, you'll make yourself ill.
ROGER. Serve her right if she does.

HELEN (*kneeling up on settee*). Oh, get away out of my sight, you pompous prig, before I lose control and smack your stupid face.
ROGER. Lose control! Ha, ha, ha! That's good, that is! Lose control! Ho, ho, ho!
HELEN (*almost shrieking, beating upon his chest with her clenched fists*). Shut up! Shut up! Shut up!
ROGER (*grabbing her wrists and holding them firmly*). That will do, Helen!

(*He breaks off with a yell as she, ducking her head, buries her teeth in his knuckles.* CEDRIC *and* SARAH *utter incoherent cries and exclamations.* CEDRIC *in particular is terribly flustered and embarrassed.*)

Ow! Let go, will you! (*Wrenching his hand away, snatching his handkerchief from his pocket and pressing it over his hand.*) You—you vicious little hell-cat, you! Look what you've done! It's bleeding. (*He crosses* R.)
HELEN (*still on the settee*). I'm glad it is! Glad!
ROGER (*between clenched teeth*). And I'm glad, too! Because it proves how utterly wrong I was just now to imagine you could ever have changed. The only difference is you're not a young fool any longer, you're a middle-aged one.

(*She gasps.*)

HELEN (*shouting him down*). Middle-aged! How dare you, you insulting swine! (*She rises and crosses* C.) How dare you! How dare you!

(ROGER *goes up to behind the table.*)

Get back to your rotten desert—if you can find one big enough to hold you—and I never want to set eyes on you again! Never! Never! Never!

(*Lightning.*)

SARAH (*while this is going on*). Stop it—at once—both of you—Helen—Roger—do you hear? Stop! Stop! Stop!

(*Thunder.* HELEN *goes* L. *in front of the armchair, snatches a book from the piano and throws it at* ROGER, *who is stalking off through the library door.*)

HELEN (*shouting*). Devil! Devil! Devil!

(*Thunder.* HELEN *crosses and scurries upstairs.*)

(*Whirling round at the top of the stairs.*) And now I'm going to the boot-cupboard, and I don't care a damn who knows it!

(*The thunder rises to a climax. She dashes off* R. *For a moment* CEDRIC *and* SARAH *stand as though bereft of speech. Then :*)

CEDRIC (*sinking into the armchair, mopping his forehead with his handkerchief*). Well, well, really—of all the appalling scenes——
SARAH (*facing him, and speaking very deliberately*). Cedric, quickly, tell me one thing : do you love me ?
CEDRIC (*taken aback by the unexpectedness of the question*). Wha——
SARAH (*louder*). Do you love me ? Because if you do (*pointing with outstretched arm to the library*) you'll go into that room now, and you'll knock that detestable man down. Hit him ! Don't bother about whether it's below the belt or not ; hit him where it's easiest—only, hard.

(*She turns, and goes quickly up stage, leaving the bewildered* CEDRIC *staring blankly.*)

CEDRIC (*rising*). But, Sarah——
SARAH (*from up stage* R.C.). Hard, Cedric !

(*She runs upstairs and exits.* CEDRIC, *with his gaze still fixed on the library door, reaches for the decanter and a glass, pours out some brandy, and, without shifting his gaze, swallows it in two or three gulps. Then, replacing the decanter and glass, he crosses to* R. *and, after a further second's hesitation, gives two peremptory raps on the library door, and strides in. At his exit, Thunder.*)

QUICK CURTAIN.

ACT III

It is about nine o'clock the next morning.
Breakfast is laid upon the refectory table, which has been moved to C. *and chairs set round. Upon the sideboard* R. *are dishes under silver covers. The room, gay and colourful with flowers and sunshine, looks charming.*

When the CURTAIN *rises,* POYNTER *is entering with tea and coffee, which he places on table; then he goes up stage, through the hall and off* R. *The next moment the sound of the gong is heard, neither very loud nor very prolonged. There is a short pause, then* HELEN, *entering the hall from* R., *comes into the room. She is wearing a skirt, blouse, and cardigan jacket, all rather carelessly put on, and her hair looks as though its morning encounter with comb and brush has been but brief and hurried. In fact, it had better be admitted at once, that* HELEN *is very, very far from looking her best. She comes down stage blinking her eyes resentfully at the sunlight, then pauses and surveys the table with great distaste. She gets a glass from the cupboard* R., *moves to the table, pours out hot water, takes aspirin and sits on the settee* R. *She sits very erect, looks at the glass with loathing, then takes a sip, gulps violently and shudders.* SARAH *is heard off singing one of those gay little French chansons which are so especially appropriate to summer mornings. Still singing, she enters the hall from* R., *pauses for a moment to glance out of the hall window, then, trilling light-heartedly, she trips down the two steps and into the room. She, in contrast to her sister, is looking particularly fresh and beautiful this morning, and entirely in the picture with the flowers and the sunshine. She carries roses in her hands, crosses to the piano and puts them in vase.*

SARAH. Good morning, dearest; good morning!
HELEN (*on the settee* R.). 'Morning.
SARAH. And isn't it the loveliest morning?
HELEN. Is it? (*She takes a sip.*)
SARAH (*stepping back*). Good heavens! that looks horribly like hot water that you're drinking.
HELEN (*wryly*). It tastes horribly like it, too.
SARAH (L.C.). My dear! (*Looking at her anxiously and taking in her appearance.*) Is anything the matter, Helen? You're not ill?
HELEN. Ill? . . . There's no need to make a fuss, Sarah, but the fact is—I'm dying.
SARAH (*looking at her, then bursting into a hearty laugh*). Non-

sense! Dying, indeed! You! (*She laughs again, then goes to the table and pours coffee for herself.*)

HELEN. Stop laughing. I've enough noise in my head for a blast furnace, without you adding to it.

SARAH. I'm so sorry, but really . . . Of course, you know what's the matter with you, don't you?

HELEN. I do.

SARAH (*at the table* R.C.). This is the reaction after that disgusting scene last night. Didn't I tell you you'd make yourself ill?

HELEN (*into her glass—as she sips*). Um!

SARAH. All that emotion and hysteria.

HELEN. And all that sherry.

SARAH (*sharply*). What? (*She moves down to* HELEN.)

HELEN. Sherry, I said. (*Pressing her hand to her forehead.*) And if you could know what your voice does to me, you'd try to make it a little less shrill.

SARAH. What sherry, dear?

HELEN. The sherry I always keep in the boot-cupboard. . . . I—I drank the whole bottle last night, Sarah.

SARAH. No!

HELEN. I did.

SARAH. You didn't!

HELEN (*peevishly*). Oh, stop arguing with me. I tell you I did. . . . I was so terrified, I had to do something or I'd have gone quite mad. (*Then weakly.*) And, anyway, I do think you might try to be a little sympathetic instead of standing there staring at me like a—like a tripper at a ruin.

SARAH. But, darling, I am terribly, terribly sorry for you. Perhaps if you were to lie down.

HELEN (*leaning back*). No, no, don't! I'd rather not——

SARAH. You poor dear! (*Striking her palm with her clenched fist.*) Oh, that man! I feel I could strangle him with my own hands! (*She moves* C. *a little.*)

HELEN. What man?

SARAH. Roger, of course! Who else?

HELEN (*closing her eyes*). Don't speak of him, Sarah.

SARAH. Of all the despicable——

HELEN (*her eyes still closed*). No, no, please! I don't want to even think of him this morning.

SARAH. If he's any vestige of decency at all, he'll have left this house hours ago. (*She sits in the chair below* C. *of the table.*)

HELEN (*opening her eyes—quickly*). Now, Sarah, I want you to be very kind and understanding, and to eat your breakfast. I'm sure it would help me enormously, darling, if you'd just be quite bright and cheerful, and—and behave as if nothing had happened.

SARAH. Of course, dearest, if you really mean that. (*Glancing longingly towards the dishes on the sideboard.*) And I am simply ravenously hungry.

HELEN. Of course you are. Go, Sarah, and eat. At once.
SARAH (*rising and crossing to the sideboard*). Well . . . I think perhaps I will. As a matter of fact, I do feel particularly bright and cheery this morning—at least, I did until I came down and found you in this state.
HELEN. I'm sure I'm very sorry to be a blot on your day.
SARAH. Don't be silly. You'll be feeling much, much better yourself presently.
HELEN (*gloomily*). I hope so.
SARAH. Of course you will. (*She lifts the covers from the dishes, humming gently to herself as she does so.*) Oh dear, oh dear, oh dear. I simply can't make up my mind whether to have fish or bacon or both.
HELEN (*faintly—sipping her hot water*). How too tiresome for you.
SARAH. The bacon looks delicious, I must say, with all those bits of kidney floating about.
HELEN (*suppressing a violent shudder*). If you love me, Sarah, you'll have fish.
SARAH. Yes. I really think I will. (*She helps herself to fish.*) Aren't you going to have anything at all?

(HELEN *shakes her head.*)

Not even a little dry toast?
HELEN. No, no.

(SARAH *pops a piece of fish into her mouth from the dish, then crosses and sits at* L. *end of the table.*)

SARAH. Oh, well, I expect you'll eat an enormous lunch.
HELEN (*sharply*). I wish you wouldn't speak with your mouth full. It's disgusting.
SARAH. Sorry, darling. My schoolgirl appetite.

(*There is a short pause, during which she continues her breakfast with very obvious enjoyment.* HELEN *glances at her once or twice, then quickly away again.*)

(*Conversationally.*) Cedric's late.
HELEN (*not interested*). Oh?
SARAH (*drinking*). Very late. (*Eating.*) I've something very important to say to my little Cedric this morning, Helen.
HELEN (*still uninterested; sipping*). Have you?
SARAH. And if he knew what that something was, he'd have been down hours ago, bless him! (*As* HELEN *does not speak.*) Hours ago, Helen.
HELEN. Hours ago would be in the middle of the night.
SARAH (*with a little laugh*). Well? Can't you think of anything I might have to say to a man that would fetch him from his bed even in the middle of the night?

E *

HELEN. Yes. Fire! (*She sips.*)

SARAH. There's no need to be peevish, dear, just because you're not feeling well.

(POYNTER *enters on the rostrum from* R. *and comes down stage.*)

POYNTER. The papers have just arrived, madam.

HELEN. Oh, put them down—anywhere, Poynter.

(*He places the papers on the piano.*)

SARAH (*as he turns to go*). Isn't Mr. Norreys up yet, Poynter?

POYNTER (*at the piano*). I really couldn't say, miss.

SARAH. Well, I think perhaps you'd better knock at his door.

POYNTER. Very good, miss.

SARAH (*delaying him again as he turns to go*). Oh—one moment. (*She rises, goes* L., *and takes a white, long-stemmed rose from the bowl on the piano.*) And I want you to give him this with my love.

POYNTER (*taking the rose from her*). Er—yes, miss.

SARAH. Now don't forget, with my love.

POYNTER. I won't forget, miss.

(*He goes up stage* C. *and off to* R. SARAH *sighs happily, sits and resumes her breakfast.*)

HELEN (*with a gesture in the direction of the hall*). And what, may I ask, is the meaning of that little ritual?

SARAH. It means, Helen, that the problem of Cedric and Sarah is solved. . . . I'm going to marry him.

HELEN. You are? Oh, I'm so glad, darling. (*She gets up, but sits again quickly.*)

SARAH (*eating her breakfast*). As soon as possible. . . . And I want you to know I shall be eternally grateful to you for everything that happened in this house last night.

HELEN. Oh!

SARAH. I didn't believe you yesterday when you described your case as exceptional. I do now. Exceptional isn't the word for it.

HELEN (*staring at her*). You mean to say it was the sight of Roger and I scratching and clawing one another that made you make up your mind to marry Cedric?

SARAH. My dear, can you imagine me and Cedric carrying on like that? The idea's absurd!

HELEN. Oh, is it?

SARAH. You were just born to fight, you two. How on earth you could have deceived yourself when he came back to you yesterday is more than I can fathom. Sentimentalizing over him, the way you did. You might have known!

HELEN. I did know.

SARAH. What?

HELEN (*rising and going to the table*). All that sentimentalizing, as you call it, was—was bogus.

SARAH. What!

HELEN (*sitting in the chair below* C. *of table, pouring out more water and taking another aspirin*). Bogus! And for your benefit. I—I thought it might help you to decide to marry Cedric if you saw us both being happy and reconciled.

SARAH (*incredulously*). But——

HELEN. Actually, if you must know, he wants me to divorce him.

SARAH. Helen! You're not serious!

HELEN. Oh, aren't I? . . . He—he wants to marry again, Sarah.

SARAH. Roger does? But—who?

HELEN. Lady Emily Willock! (*She takes another aspirin.*)

SARAH. Lady E—— . . . Not—not that revolting hag whose picture was in the " Sketch " ? Oh, no!

HELEN. Oh, yes. It seems they've been romping about in tombs together—anyway, he wants to marry her.

SARAH. But, my dear, if she's anything like that photograph——

HELEN. That's nothing to one I've seen of her on a camel. The look on that poor camel's face, Sarah!

SARAH (*shaking her head—dazedly*). But divorce! . . . You mean, none of it was real yesterday, then? (*She rises.*)

HELEN (*bitterly*). Last night was real enough.

SARAH (*going to* HELEN). But the rest . . . all that was pretending?

(HELEN *nods.*)

And you did it all for me?

(HELEN *nods again.*)

(*Kneeling beside her.*) Oh, my dear. It was very, very naughty of you, but very sweet.

HELEN. And you will marry Cedric, *won't* you?

SARAH. I'm absolutely determined to.

(*They kiss.*)

HELEN. And you'll tell him so at once?

SARAH (*going back to the table and sitting*). At the earliest opportunity. . . . It'll make him so happy. And, after all, he has been very patient. . . . You do like him, don't you?

HELEN. As much as I could like anyone this morning.

SARAH. I adore him really. . . . I wonder if he guessed when Poynter gave him that rose. I think he would, don't you? Just think! At any moment he may come bounding down the stairs, all ardent and eager, bless him! (*She gives a little self-conscious laugh as she reaches for the marmalade.*)

(HELEN *flashes her a warning look as* POYNTER, *taking* "at any moment" *as his cue, enters on the rostrum from* R. *and comes down stage. He is still carrying the rose.* SARAH *is unaware of him until he is actually beside her chair, when her laugh breaks off into a little startled exclamation :*)

Oh!

POYNTER. I knocked at Mr. Norreys' door, miss, and, as there was no reply, I ventured to look in. Mr. Norreys is not there.

SARAH. Not? . . . Oh—well—he's probably got up early and gone for a walk.

POYNTER. I don't think Mr. Norreys has been in his room all night, miss—at least, his bed hasn't been slept in.

SARAH (*with a gasp*). What? (*Then controlling herself.*)

(POYNTER *places the rose beside her on the table, then goes up stage and off to* R. *again.*)

(*The moment he has disappeared she springs up agitatedly.*) Helen—did you hear that? Cedric's not been in his room all night! (*She crosses down* R.)

HELEN. H'm! Strange.

SARAH (*hurrying round to the front of the table, her agitation increasing*). Strange! Something terrible has happened, I tell you! Oh, for God's sake, don't sit there like that! We've got to do something!

HELEN (*rises, still clutching her glass*). But—what?

SARAH (*up* L.). The police! We must telephone for them immediately!

HELEN. Don't be ridiculous, Sarah! (*She moves round to back of the table.*)

SARAH (*frenziedly*). But didn't you hear what he said? His bed hasn't been slept in! (*Wailing.*) Oh, he's dead, Helen, he's dead. Something tells me.

HELEN. Rubbish!

SARAH. Roger's murdered him! He's lying somewhere now in a pool of blood! And it's all my fault.

HELEN. Oh, pull yourself together!

SARAH (*coming down* C., *hysterically*). It is! It is! I made him do it!

HELEN (*placing her glass on the table*). Do what?

SARAH. Last night—I told him to go into that room—and thrash Roger!

HELEN. Thrash him?

SARAH. Yes, yes.

HELEN. Thrash him! Well, really, dear, that was a little foolish of you. Didn't you know that Roger won his Blue for boxing?

SARAH (*moving to* L. *of* HELEN). Don't! Oh, don't!

HELEN. But he did. Whatever his other faults may be, Roger's no weakling.

SARAH. He's a ravening murderer, that's what he is.
HELEN. Your little Cedric would never stand an earthly. Mind you, I haven't a word to say against him, dear, but there's no denying he's puny.
SARAH. Puny! Hold your tongue!
HELEN. The idea of him trying to thrash Roger; it's laughable.
SARAH. You can laugh, when Cedric may be lying dead!
HELEN. Don't be silly. He's probably only unconscious.

(*She starts to follow* SARAH, *as the latter dashes up stage.*)

Here, where are you going?

(SARAH *has crossed up* C. *and is about to go off to* R. *In the midst of the scuffle the library door opens and* CEDRIC *appears in the doorway. He is still wearing his dinner-suit, which looks extremely crumpled, his hair is tousled, and his whole appearance is that of one who has that moment been roused from a deep sleep. At the sight of him,* SARAH *and* HELEN *release one another and stare at him in dumb amazement.*)

CEDRIC (*blinking his eyes at the morning sunlight*). What's all the noise about?
SARAH. Oh, Cedric, darling! Oh, darling, you're alive! Not even hurt! (*She rushes at* CEDRIC *and flings her arms round him.*)
CEDRIC (*releasing himself*). Alive? What on earth are you talking about, Sarah?
HELEN (L.C., *quickly, coming a little down stage*). Don't take any notice of her.
CEDRIC (*noticing the breakfast-table*). Good Lord! Surely it can't be as late as all that! (*Turning and calling into the room.*) I say, Storer, it's morning.

(*There is an incoherent murmur from* ROGER, *off.*)

Oh—good morning, Helen. (*Becoming suddenly conscious of his appearance.*) I say, I'm awfully sorry. These clothes and everything. But the fact is——

(*He breaks off as* ROGER *joins him in the doorway. He also is dressed as in the previous Act. His hair, too, is tousled, and in addition his right hand is heavily bandaged with a white silk handkerchief.*)

ROGER (*also blinking a little*). 'Morning, everybody. Breakfast ready? Well, now, isn't that nice!
HELEN (*in a very rasping voice*). Will you please explain the fancy dress?
ROGER. Fancy dress! (*To* CEDRIC.) Does the old girl mean us?

(*She gives him a withering look, goes to the chair at* L. *end of the table, pulls it up* L. *and sits.*)

CEDRIC. Well, you see, the fact is——

SARAH (*above* R. *end of settee, tugging at his sleeve*). Oh, don't bother to tell us now. Do go and have your bath, darling, and then come back and eat.

CEDRIC (*hesitating, glancing at* ROGER). Well——

ROGER (*slipping his arm through* CEDRIC'S). Afraid we've no time for a bath. Have one later. Better eat now, eh? (*He marches him to the table.*)

SARAH (*staring after them*). No time?

CEDRIC. Er—he means we're so hungry, Sarah.

ROGER. Of course, old man; though I'm afraid I may have to ask you to cut up my food for me. My hand . . . (*Displaying his bandaged hand.*) You won't mind doing that for me, old man?

CEDRIC. Not at all. I'll sit next to you and help you. (*He gets the chair from below* C. *of table, and takes it round to the back.*)

ROGER (*sitting above* R. *end of table*). Thank you, old man. (*Yawning and stretching.*) By Jove, I'm as hungry as a hunter!

(SARAH *sits on the settee.*)

(*Looking down the table.*) Oh! isn't there any grape-fruit?

HELEN (*impatiently*). No, there isn't.

ROGER. Good Lord! No grape-fruit? My day's ruined.

CEDRIC (*by the sideboard, lifting covers*). A little fish, Storer? Or some bacon?

ROGER. Eh?—— Oh, fish, if you think it looks fresh.

HELEN. God give me patience! (*She rises and pushes her chair up.*)

ROGER (*pouring out coffee with his left hand*). You can't be too careful, you know. I once heard of a man who ate fish in a cheap lodging-house in Port Said—he was dead in a couple of hours.

HELEN. You're not in a cheap lodging-house now, though God knows you both look as though you ought to be.

ROGER. The doctors could do nothing for him, poor fellow. (*To* HELEN.) Yes, what were you saying, Helen?

HELEN. Oh—— (*She holds her mouth, biting her lip, then turns away to the armchair* L.C.)

ROGER (*as* CEDRIC *sets his plate before him*). Ah, thank you, old man. Now, do go and get something for yourself.

CEDRIC. Well, perhaps a little fish too.

SARAH (*rising and hurrying round to him*). No, no, darling, you sit down, and let me get it for you.

CEDRIC. Oh, but——

SARAH (*almost forcing him into his chair*). Now, darling, I insist.

CEDRIC (*submitting; sitting above* L. *end of the table, facing the audience*). Well—thank you, Sarah.

SARAH (*going to the sideboard*). Not at all.

CEDRIC (*to* ROGER, *who is on his* R.). Can you manage that fish, or shall I cut it up for you?

ROGER. I think I'd better try to manage, old man, thanks,

and get used to it. Nasty things, you know, bites. Yes, Helen, what did you say?

(*She glares at him.*)

Oh, sorry, I thought you spoke. (*He takes a fork in his left hand and proceeds to eat with exaggerated difficulty.*)

(HELEN *sits in the armchair down* L.C. SARAH *returns, places* CEDRIC'S *plate in front of him, then stands* L. *of the table.*)

SARAH. Here you are, darling. Now, have you got everything?
CEDRIC. I think so, Sarah, thank you. Oh, salt!
SARAH (*above* L. *end of table*). There it is. Now eat it quickly, darling. I've something very important to say to you.
CEDRIC (*starting to eat*). Have you, Sarah?
SARAH (*leaning over him, whispering in his ear*). Yes, about . . . you know what.
CEDRIC. Yes?
SARAH. About us, darling.
CEDRIC. Oh? Ah—well—(*to* ROGER) if you're looking for the toast, it's here. (*He passes the toast.*)
ROGER. Thanks, old man.
SARAH (*put out by* CEDRIC'S *manner*). Well, really, Cedric, you might at least try to look a little interested. I should have thought you'd be thrilled.
CEDRIC. Thrilled? Yes . . . yes, of course. (*To* ROGER.) I wonder if you'd mind passing the butter.
ROGER. Oh, my dear fellow, I'm sorry!

(SARAH, *rebuffed, steps back and stares at them both bewilderedly, then at* HELEN.)

HELEN (*explosively*). My God! If you could see yourselves sitting there in those clothes at half-past nine in the morning, wolfing like pigs!
ROGER. Pigs don't wolf. (*Displaying his bandaged hand again.*) Why, it's as much as I can do to convey a morsel to my mouth.
CEDRIC (*pausing in his eating for a moment*). Are you sure I can't help you, old man?
ROGER. No; I must try.
HELEN (*sarcastically*). I am still waiting for an explanation.
CEDRIC. Oh! You mean, why we came from the library dressed in the clothes we wore last night——
HELEN. It had crossed my mind. Well?
CEDRIC. We've neither of us been to bed. We've been in the library all night.
SARAH. But, darling, what have you been doing all night? (*She sits in the chair up* L., *vacated by* HELEN.)
CEDRIC. Doing? We haven't been doing anything. We just

sat and talked, and then we sat and slept. (*He gets on with his breakfast.*)

ROGER (*to* SARAH). Let me tell you that I think you're a bloodthirsty, thoroughly vindictive young woman. Inciting poor Norreys to go into that room and attack me, the way you did.

SARAH. Ho!

CEDRIC. I must say I hated the idea myself, Sarah.

ROGER. Thank you, Norreys.

CEDRIC. The moment I entered the room and saw him sitting there nursing his wounded hand, I knew I couldn't do it—quite apart from the fact that he's a bigger man. . . . In fact, I may say that, within five minutes, we were the best of friends.

SARAH. So it seems.

ROGER. The very best. And we're going to continue to be.

CEDRIC (*eating*). Yes, rather.

HELEN. Touching!

ROGER. Ah, you may sneer, just because you women don't understand the meaning of the word friendship.

HELEN. Shut up!

ROGER. You don't, not one of you.

SARAH (*shrilly*). Will you be quiet! Helen's not well this morning.

ROGER. Oh, is that it? I thought she was just looking her age.

CEDRIC. Anyway, we sat and talked, and I may say that I spent the most interesting few hours of my life. The most interesting.

ROGER. Very nice of you to say so.

CEDRIC. I mean it. . . . Time just slipped by. I imagine it must have been somewhere about four when we both fell asleep in our chairs.

ROGER. I believe it was later than that.

SARAH. But, darling, what on earth were you talking about?

CEDRIC. Why, Storer's work in Egypt, of course.

SARAH. Egypt?

CEDRIC. And of all the fascinating subjects I ever——

HELEN (*to* ROGER). You mean to say that you kept him up all night with your filthy Egyptology? (*She rises and then sits on the arm of the chair.*)

CEDRIC. There was no question of keeping me up, Helen. I never thought there could be anything in the world that could thrill and excite me so much. Never! Did you know, Sarah, that to build the Cheops Pyramid, two million three thousand stones were required?

SARAH (*staring at him*). I did not——

CEDRIC. Neither did I; but now that I know it, I feel that life can never be quite the same again.

SARAH (*a sharp edge to her tone*). Cedric, what do you mean?

CEDRIC. Exactly what I say. In fact, he hadn't been talking long before I realized I'd discovered the one thing my life had previously lacked.
SARAH. What?
CEDRIC. Something to be enthusiastic about. An aim, an interest and a purpose. (*He pauses.*) But I believe I explained something of it to you yesterday.
SARAH. But you told me that I meant all of that to you!
CEDRIC (*cutting her short*). And I meant every word I said.
SARAH. Then——
CEDRIC. But you kept me dangling, Sarah, you know you did.
HELEN. What's the man talking about? Dangling?
SARAH (*shrilly*). Cedric—will you please explain! (*She gets up.*)
CEDRIC. You kept me dangling too long.
SARAH. What do you mean: dangling?
CEDRIC. Just what I say: dangling!
ROGER. Damn silly of you, Sarah, and I'd have thought you were old enough to know better.
SARAH (*turning on him*). Oh, you be quiet!
ROGER. I wonder if you'd get me some more fish.
CEDRIC. Certainly, old man. (*He rises and gets fish from sideboard.*)
SARAH. Now, Cedric, I want an explanation, please!
CEDRIC. You said just now you had something important to say to me. Well, I, as it happens, have something important to say to you. . . . I'm not going to marry you, Sarah.
SARAH (*with a gasp*). Cedric! What are you saying?
CEDRIC (*crossing back to the table and sitting again*). And what's more, I'm not going to do the other thing with you, either. When Storer leaves for Egypt in three weeks' time, I shall go with him. Isn't that so?
ROGER. Of course it is, old man, and there's great work waiting for us to do out there. We're going to write a book together about the life of Queen Nefertiti.
SARAH (*inarticulate*). You . . . Egypt? . . . I don't understand. (*Turning to* HELEN.) What—what does he mean?
HELEN (*rising*). They're both drunk. (*Crossing R. to the settee.*) They've been drinking sherry all night. (*To the men.*) They ought to be ashamed of themselves.
CEDRIC (*with dignity*). We're neither of us drunk, Helen, and I'm perfectly in earnest.
SARAH. But—you can't mean—you're going to leave me? No! You're not serious?
CEDRIC. I was never more serious in my life.
SARAH. But——
CEDRIC (*with great finality*). I'm going to Egypt—with Storer.
HELEN (*by the settee R.—shrilly*). Are you trying to tell my sister you're about to jilt her for a pyramid?

CEDRIC. The pyramid was symbolic ; a mere instance. (*Glancing at his wrist-watch ; to* ROGER.) And now, don't you think we ought to be . . .

ROGER (*nodding*). Yes, quite true, old man. Ring the bell, there's a good fellow.

(CEDRIC *rises and goes* R. SARAH *and* HELEN *can only stare at him, speechless, as he presses the bell* R., *then moves a little down stage.* HELEN *sits on the settee.*)

CEDRIC. Our plans are to motor to London, bath and change at my flat, lunch somewhere or other, then start to motor to Scotland.

SARAH (*faintly*). Scotland!

CEDRIC. We shall stay at my little place there, returning in time for me to buy whatever I shall need, then sail for Egypt. (*To* ROGER.) Eh?

ROGER. I'm longing to show you the tombs.

SARAH. Cedric—oh!—you—you're joking, aren't you?

(POYNTER *enters on the rostrum from* R. *and comes down stage.*)

CEDRIC. Really, Sarah! I announce a serious decision that may affect my whole life, and you accuse me of joking. (*Clicking his tongue.*) Tck! Tck! Tck!

POYNTER. You rang, madam?

ROGER (*before* HELEN *can speak*). Yes, Poynter, I want you to see that Mr. Norreys' bags and mine are brought down and put into our cars.

CEDRIC. Coats and things too, please. (*He crosses* L.) As quickly as possible, please.

POYNTER. Very good, sir. (*He goes up stage.*)

ROGER (*calling after him*). And let us know when it's done.

POYNTER. Yes, sir.

(*He goes up to the rostrum and off to* R.)

SARAH (*as soon as* POYNTER *has gone*). Now, Cedric—you can't do this! You can't! It's unthinkable!

CEDRIC. I don't agree.

SARAH. But—but—oh, Helen, can't you say something?

HELEN (*rising—dazedly*). I can't grasp it. (*To* ROGER.) And, anyway, it's all your fault! (*She crosses to* ROGER.)

ROGER. Mine? Well, I like that!

HELEN. It is! Cedric goes into my library, possessed of all the instincts of a gentleman, spends a few hours there with you, and emerges completely demoralized: a cad, in fact!

CEDRIC. Nonsense!

HELEN (*her nerves quivering*). How dare you say "nonsense" to me! How dare you!

(CEDRIC *crosses to behind the settee.*)

SARAH (*crossing* R. *to the settee and kneeling on it*). Quiet, Helen. (*To* CEDRIC.) Cedric, if all this is because I've kept you dangling, as you call it, then I can tell you that that's over and done with. Ended. I was going to tell you this morning that I'd made up my mind to marry you. There! To marry you, Cedric, just as soon as ever you like.

CEDRIC. I'm deeply sensible of the honour you do me, Sarah, but—I'm afraid I must refuse.

SARAH (*sitting on the settee; turning away*). Oh!

HELEN (*going to her*). Darling!

SARAH (*turning to him again*). But I don't understand. Why, if I'd told you this yesterday, you'd have been wild with delight.

CEDRIC. That's true. But to-day is not yesterday.

ROGER. "Too late, too late, ah! woeful cry."

HELEN. Shut up! (*She crosses to the armchair* L.C. *and sits.*)

(*The ensuing scene between* CEDRIC *and* SARAH *is taken quickly, with* HELEN *fluttering on the outskirts, uttering occasional exclamations.* ROGER, *meanwhile, continues calmly sipping his coffee, and listening to all that is going on.*)

SARAH (*turning away with a defeated gesture and going to down* R., *on the verge of tears*). Oh, how could you ever have pretended you loved me?

CEDRIC (*behind the settee*). Now listen, Sarah; you've been on my mind ever since the first moment I met you.

(SARAH *turns to face him.*)

Oh, yes, you have. I thought of little else but you, and I don't mind confessing that some of the thoughts I caught myself thinking surprised me enormously. I'd never realized I was that kind of a man. I was in love for the first time in my life; why, if I hadn't been, do you suppose I'd have let you play fast and loose with me?

SARAH (*kneeling on the settee again*). Fast and——

CEDRIC. And loose—what else can you call it?

SARAH. But you agreed——

CEDRIC. Only because I was in such a state of abject infatuation I'd have agreed to anything. If I hadn't been, I'd have told you to go to hell! (*He crosses up to* R. *of the table. Quieter.*) All my life, Sarah, I shall be grateful to you for sending me into that room last night. Storer's descriptions of his life abroad enthralled me so much that I realized just how little it really mattered whether you married me or not.

SARAH (*rising and following him up, blazing*). Ho! I see—I don't count! You treat me abominably, and then turn round and say it doesn't matter! My God! It doesn't matter! (*She steps nearer* CEDRIC.)

ROGER (*clasping* CEDRIC'S *arm*). Look out, old man!

CEDRIC (*turning to her again*). Well, does it? (*She is speechless.*)

I mean, what happens to you and me can never be any more than trivial, compared to the fact that the Sphinx was built four thousand six hundred B.C. and is still standing. Think of that!

SARAH (*staring at him blankly, then turning to* HELEN). Helen —he's mad! (*She crosses* L. *to* HELEN.)

HELEN. Quite mad!

ROGER (*tossing his napkin on to the table and rising*). I only wish I had been as sane during a certain period of my life.

(SARAH *moves to* L. *end of settee.*)

(POYNTER *re-enters.*)

HELEN. You! As for you!
ROGER. Well?

(POYNTER *comes down stage.* SARAH *sinks down on to the settee.*)

POYNTER. The bags and coats are being put into the cars. They'll be ready when you are, sir.

ROGER. Good!

(*As* POYNTER *turns to go.*)

Thank you, Poynter, I'll see you on my way out.

POYNTER. Thank you, sir.

(*He goes up stage and off to* R.)

ROGER (*to* HELEN). As for me, Helen, what were you saying?

HELEN. I'm not well enough to think of anything bad enough. (*Rising.*) But don't imagine I'm going to divorce you. I will not. Nothing shall induce me to! So you can say good-bye to Emily. (*She crosses* R., *and sits beside* SARAH *on the settee.*)

ROGER. Emily? (*Then, recollecting.*) Oh, Emily Willock! But I thought I told you I only considered marrying her because I was so damned lonely. And now that I've got Norreys, (*slapping* CEDRIC *affectionately on the shoulder*) well, I don't expect I'll be lonely any more. Eh, old man?

CEDRIC. Why, of course you won't.

ROGER. There's no need to tell me he doesn't favour Gladys Cooper.

HELEN (*turning away with a choking exclamation*). Oh!

(CEDRIC *crosses to* SARAH *down* R.)

CEDRIC. Is it any use my saying I'm sorry?

SARAH. Sorry! (*She rises, facing front.*) Begging me to marry you one day and treating me like dirt the next!

CEDRIC. Oh, come, come!

SARAH. Like dirt! (*Crossing* L.) Not twenty-four hours ago, in this very room, you were telling me that you knew what you wanted, and now, when it's yours for the asking, you turn round and

Act III.]   LOVERS' LEAP.   79

tell me you don't want it any more. (*She sits in the armchair* L.C.) I'm not supposed even to have heard of the things I hope will happen to you.

CEDRIC (*crossing to* R. *of the armchair*). I can see it's no use trying to make you understand.

ROGER. If I might give you a parting word of advice, Sarah——

SARAH. You mayn't.

ROGER. Well, it's this: say yes or no to the next man who asks you to marry him. Don't keep him dangling, or one fine day he'll stop dangling and then, where are you?

(SARAH *ignores this, and, biting her lip, stares grimly and stonily directly in front of her.* CEDRIC, *looking down at her, fidgets uncomfortably, conscious of the difficulties of the situation, and desperately anxious to get it over.*)

CEDRIC (*at length*). Oh, well—there doesn't seem anything more to say, eh?

ROGER. And if there were, there isn't time to say it. We must be off, old man.

CEDRIC (*with increasing discomfort*). Yes. . . . Oh, well, good-bye, Sarah.

(*She does not speak.*)

Er—good-bye, Sarah.

(*She still does not speak, but continues to bite her lip and stare directly in front of her.*)

Well, anyway, you'll let me write to you, won't you? You must —yes—I—I'll write to you from Egypt, Sarah. Yes—I'll do that. (*He turns away very confusedly and bumps into* HELEN.) I beg your pardon! Oh—good-bye, Helen; and—er—thank you for a—for a——

(*Very deliberately she turns her back on him.*)

Oh, I say!—— Oh, but please——

(ROGER *catches his eye and jerks his thumb in the direction of the hall, and after another despairing look at* HELEN'S *back,* CEDRIC *turns away and starts to walk up stage. Arrived at the two steps, he pauses, one foot on the lower step, waiting for* ROGER *to join him.*)

ROGER (*to* HELEN'S *back*). Well, Helen, so it's au revoir, it seems.

HELEN (*her back still to him—very definitely*). It's nothing of the sort! It's good-bye! Good-bye, Roger.

ROGER. Never say good-bye, my dear. It's such a horrid word.

(*She stands very rigid and silent, her back to him. There is a moment of silence, then he places his hands over her shoulders, as though about to kiss the back of her neck. The next instant she has ducked her head and bitten his hand. With a sharp yelp he leaps away and rushes up stage to* CEDRIC, *holding out his hands.*)

ROGER. Oh, my God! Look what she's done now; she's bitten the other one!

CEDRIC. We'll get some iodine at the chemist.

(*They exit* L. *on the rostrum.*)

SARAH (*after a pause, speaking slowly without altering the direction of her gaze*). Mother . . . Aunt Jessie . . . Aunt Zoe . . . you . . . and now—me. Ha! Ha! Ha!

QUICK CURTAIN.

(*The* CURTAIN *rises again on the spectacle of* HELEN *and* SARAH *tucking into a hearty breakfast.*)

FINALE.

FURNITURE AND PROPERTY PLOT

Furniture set as Ground Plan.

On piano : bowl of rambler roses, 7 books in book-ends, silver rampant horse, 5 loose books, ashtray and matchbox.

On table R.C. : green glass vase of delphiniums, various illustrated periodicals, box of cigarettes, ashtray and matchbox.

On sideboard : green glass bowl standard with shade.

In sideboard : syphon, bottle of brandy, 4 glasses, various bottles of wines and spirits.

In desk : pens, ink and stand, stationery and stamps, photo of ROGER in drawer, books in small bookcase above.

On bookcase : green glass vase of roses.

ACT I

Off Stage L.
Bunch of orange-blossom with loose petals.
Suitcases.

ACT II

Off Stage L.
Salver with decanter of sherry and 4 glasses.
Tray with 4 coffee-cups, saucers and spoons, and 4 liqueur glasses.
" Evening Standard."
4 liqueur bottles, including practical brandy.

Off Stage R.
L. volume of " Encyclopædia Britannica."

ACT III

Set on table :
 4 fish-knives and forks.
 4 large knives and forks.
 4 small knives and forks.
 4 desert spoons.
 4 bread-plates.
 4 breakfast-cups, saucers and spoons.
 2 cruets.
 1 jar of marmalade.
 1 jar of butter.
 1 rack of toast.
 1 bowl of sugar with tongs.
 1 tablecloth.
 4 napkins.

On sideboard :
 1 runner.
 1 hot-plate.
 2 entrée dishes containing fish and chips, with servers.
 4 breakfast plates.

Brought in by POYNTER:
  Coffee-pot and milk-jug, practical.
  Teapot and hot-water jug.

Off Stage L.
  Red roses.
  3 Sunday newspapers.
  Aspirins for HELEN at opening.

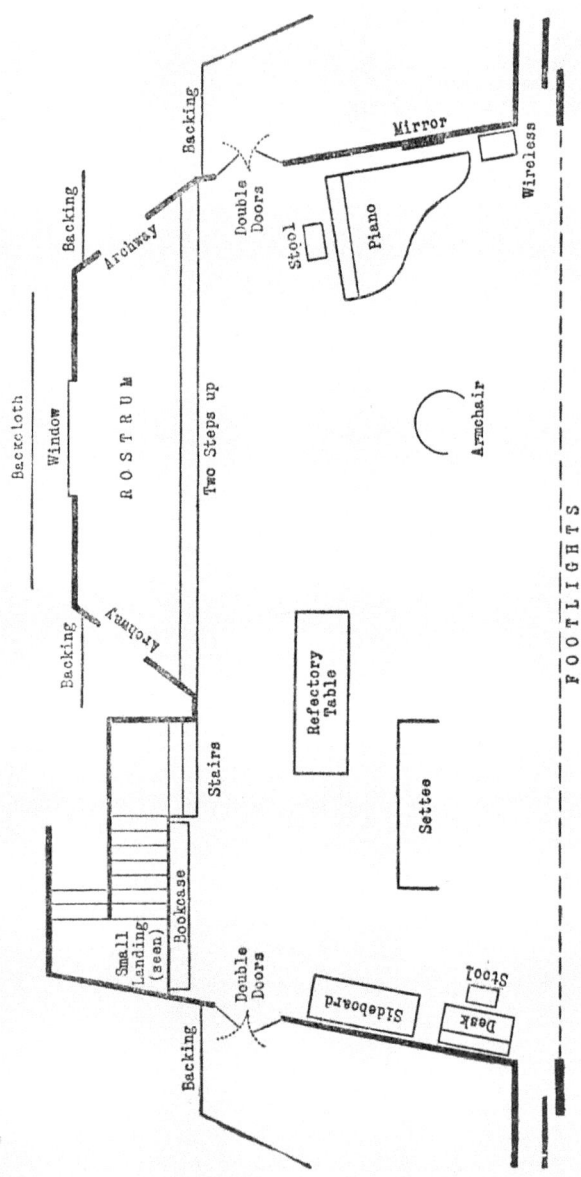

www.ingramcontent.com/pod-product-compliance
Ingram Content Group UK Ltd.
Pitfield, Milton Keynes, MK11 3LW, UK
UKHW021837210426
5322IPUK00021B/334